IVY ZELMAN

GIMME SHELTER

HARD CALLS + SOFT SKILLS FROM A
WALL STREET TRAILBLAZER

For information about this title or to order other books and/or electronic media, contact the publisher:

Aspen Gray Publishing, LLC
www.aspengraypublishing.com
kim@zelcap.com

ISBNs:
978-1-7377099-0-9 (hardcover)
978-1-7377099-2-3 (softcover)
978-1-7377099-1-6 (digital—Kindle)

Printed in the United States of America

Editorial: Stuart Horwitz, Book Architecture
Interior Design: 1106 Design
Cover Design: Taj Gaines
Author Photograph: Clint Calder

This book is dedicated to:

*Zoey, Zach and Zia, who inspire me every day
and who I love beyond words.*

David Zelman, for believing in me from the start.

My mom and dad who love me unconditionally.

Malinda Grinage, my soul mate, who I miss every day.

Ally Wesley, my palsy forever and ever.

*Kim Gray, Dennis McGill, Alan Ratner—you are my closest
inner circle and I am beyond grateful to have you in my life.*

And a special thank you to:

Jeanette McMurtry, for encouraging me to write this book.

*Stuart Horwitz, my book editor, who put up with my endless
changes without ever showing his frustration.*

*The Walker & Dunlop Team: Susan Weber, Chris Zegal, Addy Burr,
Madison Bridges, Taj Gaines and Matt Cabral.*

Table of Contents

Foreword

by Steve Eisman
Senior Portfolio Manager, Neuberger Berman

I first started talking to Ivy Zelman a few years before the great financial crisis. She was a sell-side analyst at Credit Suisse covering home builders, and from the start it was clear that she was unusually gifted. Most sell-side analysts are timid—too scared to make a negative call on their sector because they fear management will cut them off. Also, if an analyst makes a negative call on their sector and they are wrong, it is often a career-ending event.

Ivy, on the other hand, has guts. She made a negative call on the home builders way before the financial crisis began and took a lot of flak for it, at least at first. Of course, she was eventually proven correct, but it was not easy. For that she has my deepest respect.

I have been in the investing business for a long time, both on the sell side and the buy side. Ivy is one of the most remarkable analysts I have ever come across. She can both pick stocks and produce original research, which is a very unusual combination.

Her unique perspective on our world of Wall Street shines through the pages of *Gimme Shelter*—I know you're going to enjoy it.

Preface

YOU CAN HANDLE ANYTHING

When I first set out to write this book, I was driven by a desire to share the story of how I succeeded on Wall Street against the odds, in the hopes that an honest and open account would prove helpful to young adults pursuing their dreams with the same determination I felt so many decades ago. While that is certainly still my aim, I have sold a controlling interest in the firm I founded since first putting pen to paper. I am thrilled that through the new partnership with Walker & Dunlop and their incredible platform, I have secured the legacy that I worked so hard to build. The shift renewed my urgency to finish this project; arriving at such a significant milestone in my career made chronicling what went into getting to this point take on a new poignancy.

When I decided to leave my secure job at Credit Suisse—a large bulge bracket Wall Street firm—to start my own research boutique, I underestimated the amount of work it would take to accomplish the successful transition. That didn't matter though; I was powered by excitement and passion. I couldn't turn my brain off, so I often found myself up at three o'clock in the morning in those early days, drawing from pure adrenaline to fire on all cylinders. With the help of my husband, David, and Dennis McGill, my cofounder, as well as a handpicked team of others I trusted equally as much, we began to build the business piece by piece. It's all a blur looking back, as I hammered out the logistics of launching a new business while traveling constantly and raising three kids under the age of seven to boot. I was undoubtedly overwhelmed, but I was also thrilled beyond reason.

At the time we launched Zelman & Associates, the housing crisis was unfolding. My team and I had called the top of the market in 2005, and we opened our doors in October of 2007, just months after the housing market had officially begun its crash in March of that same year. Every morning, David and I would scour the *Wall Street Journal* trying to absorb the latest in the series of disasters happening in the financial world. The scale of the crisis taking shape was shocking, but it was exhilarating to know that our new firm was on center stage. We had instant credibility from being right about the massive risk in the housing market, but we also knew you're only as good as your last trade and so we remained focused on the future. Our goal was to help our clients navigate the turbulence and forecast how and when the housing market would recover.

And that's exactly what we did. We called the bottom of the market in January 2012 and proceeded to introduce timely thematic research on the single-family rental market in 2011—*Leasing the American Dream*—and outlined how mortgage credit would return to normal in *Great Unwind*, our April 2014 publication. Zelman's comprehensive reports, along with our monthly and quarterly surveys, provided our institutional and corporate partners the insight necessary to make strategic investments and manage their stock portfolios. Now, nearly fifteen years later, I have found the right partner to carry my vision yet further as we aim to broaden our end market beyond Wall Street by capitalizing on Walker & Dunlop's leading commercial real estate platform. I can't help but pause here to take a deep breath, my first in many years, and reflect on how I got here.

Looking back, I see that my career, my college education, my teenage years, my childhood, it all played an integral part in where I ended up. My career trajectory and the success of Zelman & Associates was made possible through the hundreds of moving pieces of my life coming together just right.

As silly as it may sound, my childhood brawls, adjusting to an abrupt relocation to England for my dad's job at the age of twelve—which I did in stride, roaming the streets of London and riding the tube with my new friends without any parental oversight—negotiating my way backstage at rock concerts as a teenager, all worked together to prepare me to boldly stride into my professional life. One by one, these experiences were planting the seeds for my future success.

It wasn't easy. There were many barriers; some of which can be expected on any career path, and some which struck without warning and left me flat on my back. But each time I climbed back onto my feet and pressed onward. I readjusted my approach, keeping a lower center of gravity. I grounded myself with friendships that have held strong through the decades and by building a family with my husband, David.

Along the way, I was also helped by many people who seemed to pop up to play a short but significant role in my growth: the gentleman who interviewed me as a favor which became the turning point of my career; the founder who met me for dinner and gave me the final push I needed to strike out on my own; and those who gave me affirmation that I was right to stick to my guns when it mattered most.

I am ready to move into the next phase of my journey as part of Walker & Dunlop; but even as I embrace change and welcome certain parts of the business morphing and expanding, I am gratified to know that my passion for helping others in the way I have been supported throughout my career will remain a constant. I want to be the unexpected source of wisdom, the person who takes the time to tell you what you need to hear, and the one who hands you the tools you need to know what to do with it. More than anything else, though, I hope you close this book for the last time trusting that when things get hard, you have what it takes to handle anything that stands in your path.

Chapter One

FOLD SOME TOWELS
(AND TAKE CONSTRUCTIVE CRITICISM)

"I get dizzy just talking to you, Ivy."

One of my most vivid memories from childhood took place on the floor of my mother's bedroom one warm summer afternoon. It was the summer of 1973 and I was seven years old, sprawled across the carpet in my best bathing suit with my multicolored mutt, Cinnamon, by my side, watching my mother make her bed. After a morning of playing in the sun outside, I was ready to talk business. I told my mother that someday I would own Mattel. It was one of the few companies I was aware of at such an early age, but it wasn't about Mattel really. I had simply decided I was going to be successful when I grew up, and I wanted my mom to know it. She looked down at my tiny frame and messy auburn hair and let out a little laugh. "Sure, honey. That sounds good."

A few years into my schooling at that point, it was becoming clear I was an average student—aside from in math, that is. Well into middle and high school, I was a standout when it came to numbers. But in all subjects, whether or not I had a natural aptitude, I was relentlessly curious. Most memories of my classroom interactions are of teachers sighing, and my classmates rolling their eyes as I blurted out a question midlesson or interrupted someone to ask, "But why?" or "How?" or "What about this?" I felt compelled to be an active participant. On the rare occasions my questions ran out, I was quick to make sure my opinions were known and was rarely subtle or discreet about it. Yet somewhat inexplicably, my teachers tended to love me even as they endured my smartass outbursts—most of the time. There was, of course, the college professor who threw an eraser at my head when I pointed out he got something wrong in the formula he had written on the board.

As I neared the end of high school, I realized I wouldn't be able to walk forward on the traditional path that so many other students take. I knew I wanted to continue my formal education, but I also had no choice but to embrace what I thought of as real life. To this end, in 1984, I cut my senior year short, graduating six months early to begin working for my dad in Queens while also taking night classes in New York City at Baruch College. The city was my campus, and I adored the electric energy that pulsated around me. It was at Baruch that I met my dear friend, Elena, in an introductory course to Western Civilization. The moment I walked into the classroom and first laid eyes on her, I knew I wanted to be friends. Elena and I clicked instantly. She was the Cypriot version of me: fun, loud, and definitely annoying at times. In one math course, our exasperated professor had us sit on opposite sides of the room. Our constant chatter never stopped, and he assumed our whispering meant we were cheating. He was wrong; we just had a lot to say to each other. Even when separated, we both maintained our As.

Elena was one of the friends who helped me take full advantage of the incredible nightlife New York City had to offer, something I was unwilling to miss out on despite my heavy course load and forty-hour work weeks. It felt good to be earning money while also pursuing my education, and I wanted to make sure to enjoy the aspects of the city that this opened to me. Elena played a big part in that, teaching me which brands were the very best in skincare, makeup, and couture clothing. More important at the time, she taught me how to find these things at a bargain. We'd scour the aisles at Century 21, a large discount department store near the World Trade Center, picking up many things we couldn't afford and dreaming about the day we'd be able to take home whatever luxuries we wanted. After a long day of shopping, we would often head to one of our favorite Greek restaurants, where there was live bouzouki music, dancing, and the breaking of plates.

Even while making sure to embrace life in New York City, my study habits improved dramatically while at Baruch in a shift I attribute to two main factors. Firstly, I was finally at the stage in my education where I was able to drill down into my chosen area of study. Sticking with my talent for numbers, I followed in my father's footsteps and pursued a degree in accounting—a choice which pairs neatly into my second driver; I was determined to land an incredible job after my studies. Choosing a solid major, accepting nothing less for myself than straight As, and making sure to outstrip the other students in my course were all part of this endeavor. Once I got my degree, I didn't want to waste time finding my way onto the successful career path I had envisioned for myself since being a scrappy seven-year-old.

It might sound crass, but I wanted to be rich. The future I dreamt of was one in which I was fully self-sufficient and never had to worry about my financial security. We all have our own reasons for wanting to succeed. By the time I enrolled at Baruch, I had known what it was to be comfortable, and I had learned how it felt to stretch every dollar and still come up short. As a child, my family's financial situation was solid. Looking back, I realize we were slightly above middle class at best, but as far as I was concerned, we were rich. And I see now how the sense of security that it gave me allowed my dreams of the future to roam free of fear.

The stability of that era of my life came from my father's role as CFO of London America, an import/export company owned by Midland Bank. I regarded my father, Norman Schneider, in awe, and it seems clear now that my bold claim I would someday own Mattel was almost surely influenced by my visits to his office. Around that same age of seven, I occasionally started accompanying my father to work with my older sister, Caryn. On the commute, we'd sit quietly watching our father read the *Wall Street Journal* with his legs crossed and his handsome face creased in concentration. When our excitement won out and we couldn't help but interrupt, he'd patiently show us how to carefully fold the pages of the paper so as not to disturb the people around us. The first leg of the journey was on the Long Island Railroad before we transferred to Grand Central Station and then had to hustle deep underground to catch the subway. It was crowded and intimidating, but my father would clutch each of our hands tightly from our descent onto the platform to our ride on the biggest escalator I had ever seen which brought us back up onto the streets of New York City.

His office was in Midtown, on Madison and 52nd Street, right in the center of the skyscraper capital of the world. Even as a young girl, I was impressed by his thirtieth-floor office. One whole wall was a window with a ledge big enough for both my sister and me to sit on. From that perch, I could see people milling around like ants far below in one direction and my father settling behind his massive mahogany desk in the other. I'd study him from my spot by the window, taking in his thick black hair, his warm brown eyes, and his strong jaw. A man like him belonged in an office like this, I remember thinking. He exuded a strong sense of command, and I couldn't help but burst with pride.

As a new college student, this image of my father is what I held in my mind. I wanted to end up behind the big, important desk, secure in the knowledge that what I was doing was good and what I was doing was important. My father's success was tied to his discipline which was present in all aspects of his life, not simply work. His commute may have been two hours at best, sometimes three, but he never failed to get an early-morning exercise in—a habit which was almost unheard of in the seventies. When he got home from work, no matter how late, he'd make time for my sisters and me. Depending on the time, he'd take Caryn, Ally, and me to the park or help us with our homework or chase us around with the bug we needed him to kill for us while we shrieked with laughter. As the toughest of his three girls, I was taught by my dad how to break in a mitt as well as how to throw and hit balls. He modeled what a healthy and successful life beyond just work looked like for me, and I was hungry for the lessons.

The life I had grown accustomed to changed dramatically in my high school years. The United States entered a severe recession which greatly impacted my father's company. His disciplined commitment to his work and his family gave way to distractions and stress. The mounting pressure resulted in my parents separating and, after a childhood of financial and emotional security, I suddenly found myself effectively operating on my own. Whether I liked it or not, my transition to adulthood came early.

It was a challenge to adjust to my independence during such a pivotal time. I didn't have a parent to shepherd me through the college application process. No one was there telling me how to prepare for the SAT, explaining what I should be looking for in a university, or taking me on campus tours. One Friday during my senior year, a friend of mine mentioned she was taking the SAT the next day and suggested I should too. I showed up without knowing what the test was or why it mattered. Perhaps unsurprisingly, I didn't do well. When I applied to one college, The State University of New York at Albany, I submitted a hastily handwritten application done in one sitting without reading over any of my answers a second time. I didn't get in.

Abruptly, the dreams of success I had fostered since childhood took on a sense of urgency. I enrolled at Baruch College. I had decided that figuring the future out by myself did not mean I wasn't going to make it—only that it was going to be a longer journey. I committed to my studies with an intensity that bordered on obsession. After a year of working for my dad and taking night classes at Baruch, in early 1985, I transferred to Northern Virginia Community College before settling in to finish my degree in May of 1990 at George Mason University. Through the years and moves across state lines, I had never once doubted that I'd finish my degree. However, as the end neared, I began to wonder if accounting, while safe, was the right career choice for me after all.

Life at Arthur Young

The uncertainty crept in during the final two years of my education. I was taking night classes at George Mason while also working eight to five every day as a secretary at Arthur Young & Co., now part of Ernst & Young. I was not self-conscious that it was taking me six years to complete a four-year degree; I had been working full-time since graduating early from high school, and I was proud that I was pragmatic, gritty, and somehow making it all work. Accepting the position at Arthur Young & Co. was part of this strategy. I had gravitated to the job for the same reason I had selected every role I held during my school years—the company offered tuition reimbursement.

While that was undoubtedly the deciding factor, there were other aspects of the job that initially appealed to me. From the physical building itself to the vibe inside the office, Arthur Young felt like a truly professional environment. I had worked as a temp before and often seemed to find myself in rundown buildings far outside the boundaries of town. Pulling into the private Arthur Young parking lot bordered by lush hedges, before walking the short distance into the new stand-alone office, provided a stark contrast and one I liked. I felt surrounded by success and was optimistic about what it meant for my personal journey.

To my surprise, my enthusiasm for the new role didn't seem to earn me many friends. I would make my way through the pile of work assigned to me with laser focus before beelining back to the desk of the head secretary, Glenda, to ask, "What's next? What can I do?" It was only a few weeks in when another secretary who was a few years older than me roughly pulled me into the bathroom. It was clear she was angry, even just from the way she was standing far closer to me than was socially acceptable. The intention was to intimidate. "You need to slow the hell down," she hissed, right into my face. "You're making us all look bad." Then, she was gone. The bathroom door swung shut with a crash behind her, and I was left to gape alone at the sink.

It didn't feel good to know the other secretaries didn't like me, but the approval of my peers mattered to me far less than making the most of my new role. It wasn't just about the work ethic I had developed from supporting myself over the past several years; emotionally, personally, I loved the feeling of throwing myself fully into a project before tackling the next. I felt like I was finally getting a true taste of what postgraduate life would be like. I would eavesdrop on the accountants talking in their offices near my desk and later bombard them with questions: "Do you like your job? Are you happy? Do you think I'd make a good accountant? What should I look for in a firm?" I wasn't here to make friends. I was here to work toward a better future.

I seemed to have better luck connecting with the accountants than my fellow secretaries. One in particular took a genuine interest in me and was always game to field my rapid-fire questions, even as he would laugh and say, "I get dizzy just talking to you, Ivy."

His name was Terry Lloyd. Somehow, this married Mormon from Utah decided he wanted to coach a young Jewish upstart from Long Island. It may have been an unlikely pairing but Terry, with whom I am still friends to this day, says he saw a rare passion in my eyes, and he knew I would go far. It's only fitting that he was the one who broke the news to me: "You don't want to be an accountant, Ivy."

I knew in my gut that he was right, but I didn't want to believe him. For the past six years of my life, I had dedicated my academic efforts toward becoming an accountant. I was months away from it becoming official. The thought that had all been in vain was devastating. "So what am I going to do then?" I finally managed to get out.

Terry proceeded to give me life-changing analysis: "In accounting, all you do is look at history. As an auditor, you're examining what already happened. You're searching for mistakes and irregularities, expenses that weren't properly entered, and making sure the books are correct. On top of that, auditors make people nervous so everyone else in the office tends to avoid them. Accountants get used to rooms full of nothing but books and paperwork. There isn't much interaction with other people, which is something that you, Ivy, need with all that energy and ambition you've got."

Terry knew me. He had taken the time to watch how I worked, learn what excited me, and process my background. As our friendship progressed, he had come to understand how much financial security and achievement meant to me.

"You need a job where you focus on the future," he said. "There are lots of those careers in finance. Which is good news for you because finance is where you want to be if you want to get rich." He laughed, watching my face change.

"You should get a job on Wall Street."

While this was the clearest it had been said to me, it actually wasn't the first time I had heard that I'd be better suited to a career in finance than one in accounting. Over my two years at Arthur Young, I had sought feedback on my strengths, interests, and career-path trajectory from everyone I came across who had more experience than me. I closely listened to their input, sure, but I also heard the things they didn't say and studied their actions from the sidelines. I knew Terry was right. Accounting was not for me.

It was too late to change majors and pursue finance in a classroom setting, so I threw myself into learning as much about "The Street" as I could on my own time. I scoured the library for anything relevant, pulling *Den of Thieves, Barbarians at the Gate*, and *Liar's Poker* down from the shelves. If it had to do with Wall Street, I read it. I didn't stop there, however, also finding and tearing through copies of annual reports from the biggest companies on Wall Street at the time, like Salomon Brothers and Merrill Lynch.

I was driven by near frantic energy. I thought of the last six years of putting myself through school, driving my beat-up, white 1984 Toyota Corolla all over New York and then Northern Virginia. I thought of getting up early when everyone else my age was still sleeping off a night of partying to fit in my studies, the many jobs I held, and the grocery shopping and bill paying. I thought about how I kept my house clean and organized for myself and my boyfriend, Ian, with little help beyond the occasional call with my mother to get an easy recipe so I could put dinner on the table. I had come too far and invested too much to settle for a career that wasn't right for me. I was going to get the best job possible.

Do You Know Anyone on Wall Street?

It was exhausting, but I was getting good at taking care of myself in all facets of life. I would rush from work to class, only to come home and install blinds over our back sliding doors. My boyfriend, Ian, and I lived in a Section 8 townhouse with paper thin walls and terrible insulation. We were perpetually either too hot or too cold. Because electricity was included in our rent but not gas, I used to heat the kitchen where I studied at our little table for two by turning on the oven. I spent most of my "free time" hunched over my books at that table—unless, of course, I was out buying a couch for our home at bargain basement prices.

The pace and condition at which I was living threatened to become unsustainable many times. The grind was everywhere—at school, at work, at home. But Ian was my rock. I first laid eyes on him on a street in Queens. I was nineteen, and I dubbed it love at first sight. He was gorgeous, with Greek and American Indian ancestry and a sculpted body. When he moved back to Northern Virginia, I decided I'd move there too without a moment's hesitation. I couldn't have known it then, making an impulsive decision as a lovestruck teenager, but that move very likely changed the course of my life.

As I entered my twenties, I was presented with the invaluable opportunity of a fresh start in a new place. I strode into the next decade of my life with Ian by my side as a strong and steady stabilizer. I also quickly befriended Peggy Hurley, the girlfriend of Ian's best friend, and a woman who went on to become a beloved and reliable source of support as well. With the benefit of these meaningful relationships and no longer being hampered by my involvement in the party scene, I found that I was able to drill down on my schoolwork with a new level of determination. Ian never wavered in encouraging me, supporting me and, most important, reminding me that there was more to life than getting good grades. Once when I worried I had failed an important test, Ian had me lay on a blanket on a warm summer night to look at the stars. But even as I appreciated his constant reminders to find a healthy perspective, I couldn't help but strive for perfection.

I was always scheming about how I could combine the various things I needed to get done to get through my weeks more efficiently. Sometimes, the multitasking failed, like when I tried to cram my required textbook readings into red lights on my drives to school or work. Sometimes, though, it worked better than I could have hoped. For example, when I wanted to join a health club but couldn't afford it, I asked the director if I could work for the club in exchange for a free membership and he agreed. My daily routine expanded to include early mornings spent in the gym's laundry room washing and drying towels. While a cycle was running, I was able to get in a good hour or two of studying before I had to fold. Then, I went upstairs, exercised, and showered before heading to work at Arthur Young.

While wildly efficient already, that still wasn't enough for me. I was in the midst of deciding my future was on Wall Street when I suddenly found myself exercising side-by-side with the kind of people who could actually afford a fancy gym membership, without having to barter manual labor for it. The exposure to a new, higher level of professional was too valuable not to capitalize on. Meaning every time I ventured upstairs after finishing the laundry, I'd ask anyone and everyone I came across: "Do you know anyone on Wall Street?"

I have always been comfortable with networking; from very early in my life, I understood that it is a crucial component of success. I know many people may feel awkward about it at first, but it's necessary to get over any embarrassment or reluctance to ask people for help. I think my willingness to embrace networking was formed, in large part, from seeing the way my mother interacted with others in my childhood. We'd walk into the grocery store, and I'd watch her absolutely commandeer the space. She had made sure that everybody there knew her and that they loved her, and, because of this effort, we were invited to cut lines, we got the best cuts of meat, and we kids were handed free pickles to snack on. My mother knew how to get what she needed; she was loud and efficient, yes, but also charming enough to pull it off with a certain kind of grace. I couldn't have known it as a child but mirroring her people skills was going to prove crucial to my future success.

Over the course of my career, from folding towels until now, I have found that people are generally willing to help those who are vulnerable, hungry, and humble. To this day, I remain a queen networker both professionally and personally, and cannot emphasize enough the way it has benefited me, my family, and my friends.

After many fruitless chats with many sweaty gym goers, I finally found someone with a connection. This man had a friend, C. J. DeSantis, at Merrill Lynch and he agreed to set up an informational interview for me. I was excited, but I also maintained realistic expectations. I knew better than to expect a job offer. Informational interviews are about allowing new industry entrants to pick a qualified professional's brain, hear about their experience, and learn how they can prepare to enter that field. While such a meeting with C. J. DeSantis would certainly be valuable, I had had several informational meetings already at that point which had left me deeply frustrated.

A theme had united each of those experiences. Toward the end of my informational interview at Dean Witter, the woman I met with told me: "You're not the typical candidate that we usually hire . . ." I left her office at the top of the World Trade Center pretending not to know what she meant, but I was again confronted by it when a woman at Prudential put it more bluntly: "We have a lot of Ivy League students coming in here and we only recruit at the best schools. Your story, while good . . . well, I want to be honest with you. I don't know that you have what it's going to take to make it at one of these firms."

I felt deflated as I worried that elitism alone was going to bar my way onto Wall Street, but I remained resolute in my confidence that I would be an asset to any firm. No, I didn't come from money or have a last name with built-in contacts. Sure, it took me six years to finish a four-year degree. But I felt an ironclad assurance that I had even more reason to be proud of myself for getting my degree and persevering with very little help, and against the odds.

My Big Break

As my meeting with C. J. DeSantis drew closer, another opportunity presented itself—and this time, it was an actual job interview. The managing partner at Arthur Young, Dave Wilson, had put my name forward for a role at Salomon Brothers in New York. Salomon was a big client of Arthur Young, and Dave's recommendation carried a great deal of weight due to his seniority within the company. He was my boss's boss and while he was always warm and friendly when we made small talk in the hallway, I was shocked he would go out of his way to help me to such an extent. But it seemed he was drawn by my ambition and tenacity as he told the recruiter at Salomon: "You need to meet this young lady. She's really special."

Efficient as always, I decided to schedule the formal job interview on the same day as my informational one already on the books. I would see C.J. DeSantis at 11:00 a.m. and walk the few blocks to Salomon Brothers for my 2:00 p.m. appointment. I put on the Burberry suit my surrogate mother, Jayne, and I had found on super sale for the occasion. Jayne Sigmon was my friend's mother who pretty much adopted me when her daughter enlisted in the Navy. Jayne needed a daughter and I craved her love and support. That morning, I remember feeling dressed up and professional, although I can't help but laugh now when I think back on how conservative the outfit was—nothing at all like I would wear today.

I walked into the meeting with C. J. knowing that he was a vice president and that he worked in fixed income, but little else. I wasn't sure exactly what it was that he did aside from knowing he worked with bonds. The interview took place in a conference room where we sat comically far from each other across a long stretch of table. While C. J. was an average-sized man, he gave off a confident and somewhat brusque aura. You could tell immediately he was someone who had little time to waste.

He jumped right in. "Why do you want to work on Wall Street?" Hardly pausing, he asked, "What is it specifically that you're interested in?"

I took a breath. "Well, I'm trying to get a job in investment banking."

"Do you have any interviews set up?"

"Yes," I said proudly, "I actually have an interview today at two o'clock at Salomon Brothers."

"Really?" C. J. finally paused for a moment. I could practically see the wheels in his head turning. "What can you tell me about Salomon Brothers?"

"Um, well, the CEO is John Gutfreund," I offered, saying his last name as gut-friend.

He cut me off there. "It's pronounced good-friend."

C.J. was talking loud, almost yelling. Although part of me shrank back from the energy, I thought I could detect that it wasn't coming from a place of anger, but from wanting me to succeed.

"Where's your *Wall Street Journal*?" he asked. "Did Salomon have a tombstone in there today?"

I looked at him blankly. I didn't know what a tombstone even was, and I certainly didn't have a *Journal* with me. I was studying for an international marketing exam, and all I had in my briefcase were my notes.

He carried on, undeterred. "A tombstone is an announcement a firm makes when it does something major, like issuing debt, or going public. They get their name from the shape of the message. You better get yourself a newspaper before your interview and see if Salomon did a deal."

"I will!" I promised. "I will!"

C. J. then asked me a few questions about my background, but it seemed like he knew the gist already: I was going to night school while working full-time, and I was getting ready to use my state-school degree to try to get a job in an Ivy League world. He didn't mince his words, telling me how hard it was going to be; if I wanted to beat out candidates from more prestigious schools, I was going to have to work that much harder.

As our meeting began to wind down, C. J. offered me insight on the difference between Salomon Brothers and Merrill Lynch. Merrill Lynch was considered the muscle of Wall Street, he said, while Salomon was seen as the brains. I wrote down every word coming out of his mouth. I wanted to prove I was a quick study and absorb the valuable information he was giving me. Instead of rushing his way through an informational interview that offered him nothing, C. J. was taking the time to arm me with the knowledge I'd need to make the most of my upcoming appointment at Salomon Brothers. Realizing that this Wall Street VP saw something in me that made him root for my success was exhilarating. I knew how valuable these minutes he was giving me were, and I resolved not to let him down.

This is what I had been hungry for. It didn't matter that C. J. was lecturing me or had even raised his voice at parts. I could easily put my feelings aside. For as long as I can remember, I've tried to gracefully accept constructive criticism. You can call it flexibility, or humility, but I see it as little more than a practical tool. Good advice is hard to come by, and it doesn't matter what tone it's delivered in. If I wasn't as prepared for Wall Street as I thought—and that seemed to be what C. J. was saying—then I wanted to be told that.

C. J.'s voice softened as we stood up from the table.

"You're going to do great," he said as he walked me out the door.

I literally ran from the office, desperate to pick up a *Wall Street Journal* before my 2:00 p.m. meeting. I flipped to the tombstone section and saw pages and pages of densely packed deal announcements. I was uncomfortably aware of each minute sliding by, but I did my best to work my way through the massive amount of information. Finally, I spotted it—UPS had done a senior note offering for $200 million and Salomon Brothers was the underwriter. I closed the paper, muttering to myself: "Thank God. Thank God. Thank God."

Ironically, I ended up being ready for my interview with an hour to kill. I took a deep breath and felt a kind of peace wash over me. I remember strolling to the Salomon Brothers' corporate offices, calm enough even to notice how beautiful the day was. While still nervous,

I felt confident and more in command of myself and how the next few hours would go than I could have imagined even just that morning.

The afternoon was full and passed quickly as I found myself shuffled from office to office for a series of short, fast-paced interviews. Finally, I found myself sitting in front of Kirk Meighan, an associate in corporate finance in the Transportation group. He asked me: "Why do you want to work at Salomon Brothers?"

I took a deep breath and then started. "Well, while Merrill Lynch might be the muscle of Wall Street, Salomon Brothers is the brains . . ."

I regurgitated much of what C. J. had told me mere minutes earlier, making sure to weave in aspects of my own story and information I had learned from my Wall Street self-education of the past several months. He was courteous as he walked me out of his office saying, "I look forward to having a follow-up."

I thanked him and paused by the door. "Oh, by the way," I said. "I understand that Salomon Brothers did a senior note offering for UPS. Congratulations."

Kirk looked stunned, and it was hard to read his expression behind the thick glasses he was wearing. Then his face broke into a broad smile, and he put his hand to his heart. "Oh my god, that was my deal. Thank you."

In that moment, I knew I had the job—and I was right. I left New York two days later with a formal offer to join Salomon Brothers' two-year financial analyst program.

Chapter Two

DEFEND YOURSELF
(BUT DON'T BE OVERSENSITIVE)

"I really like your outfit today, Ivy."

I have never been delicate. I spent a lot of my childhood hanging with the boys, doing whatever it was they were doing whether that was playing sports, collecting and trading baseball cards, or occasionally playing with matches (and making sure to put out the small fires we started, of course). My mom found herself in a constant battle trying to get me to bathe as a tween. As she was dragging a brush through the snarls of my long auburn hair on a particularly combative day, she decided she had had enough. She took me to the hairdresser the next morning, where I was given a nonoptional bob that made me cry.

I may have hated how it looked, but it was a strategic haircut for a girl who found herself in as many fights as I did. Whether I was brawling with my sisters at home, challenging the bullies at school, or standing my ground against the tough girls on my street, I continued to ignore the many adults asking me to please, please just use my words. I certainly don't condone fighting, but my willingness to stand up for myself and my friends when we were wronged, regardless of who we were up against or what might happen in return, instilled within me a certain brand of bravery I carried into the male-dominated world of Wall Street. I had developed a thick skin, and I thought I could handle any situation.

Most of my thoughts on being a woman working on Wall Street were formed long after I took my first role at Salomon Brothers. At that point, it hadn't even crossed my mind that being a woman could be considered a handicap. It seemed to me that everyone who joined the Salomon Brothers' training program had to work incredibly hard to survive, regardless of their gender. Sure, there were only three women in the group of seventy, but the experience was brutal for all of us I thought. We worked long hours, starting our days at 8:00 a.m. and wrapping up by 10:00 p.m.—if we were lucky—and we were expected to get work done on the weekends too. We scoured financial statements, built spreadsheets, and prepared pitch books under ridiculous deadlines. The work often required us to meticulously input numbers, sometimes with senior people looming over us, micromanaging our work.

The contrast between Arthur Young (AY) and Salomon Brothers was obvious from the start. If my boss at AY handed me an assignment on a Friday afternoon, which I handed back on Monday, he'd be grateful for my hard work. When I was handed a Friday afternoon assignment at Salomon, on the other hand, I stayed until I finished even if it meant pulling an all-nighter. If the finished product had a mistake, an AY executive would say, "Hey, great job on this. There were a few calculations that you didn't run properly . . ." But Salomon was a 100 percent error-free environment. There was one right way to do everything, all the way down to acceptable font size, and any deviation could land you in big trouble. To this day, I attribute my insane attention to detail to this environment.

"Ivy, where the fuck are you?" was a common opening line from a superior who needed me when I wasn't at my desk. This was no ordinary nine-to-five job. I could sit at my desk for hours at a time, into the next day even, waiting for some senior person to review a pitch book when he—they were nearly all *hes* in those days—might be home having dinner with his family only turning to the work at his convenience, before sending it back to the office via a car service. There was no leaving early. It was simply never discussed as an option.

While sexism at Salomon Brothers wasn't immediately obvious to me as I said, I couldn't help but notice the double standard at times. I witnessed a real men's locker room vibe, where the managing directors would turn blind eye to the lateness of young male analysts who stumbled in hungover, as long as they had good enough war stories from the night before that they were willing to share. I was never the recipient of such goodwill, nor were the other women alongside me.

The training program was a two-year grind steeped in internal competition. Each analyst strained to be seen as the best in their class as nearly everyone had the same goal; after completing the training program, they would head off to business school having made such a great impression that they would surely be offered an associate position from Salomon upon their graduation. The intensity was palpable; the program was clearly designed to weed out the weak. Performance was everything, and it was necessary to excel even in the face of exhaustion, intimidation, and blatant favoritism.

We Should Grab Dinner

Given this context, it feels necessary to directly address the sexism I began to feel and how I responded to it in the hope there is something of value for others to take away from my experience. First, I want to reiterate that it's just that: my experience. Over time, I developed certain strategies and drew specific lines as I advanced in my career, and I felt out what behavior was acceptable to me in the workplace and what was clearly inappropriate. This is a process every woman needs to carry out for herself. I am not someone who paints a picture of workplace discrimination, or the right response to it, with a broad brush.

I have always known that being sensitive will not get me where I want to go. From the time I first worked in an office, I realized I didn't have the energy to waste on being offended if a man looked at me a beat too long or made an uncomfortable joke in my presence. I thought that letting what felt like small things roll off my back would enable me to focus on my work. I would instead reserve my fury for what I considered the ultimate form of sexual harassment: men using their position of power to purposefully push physical or romantic contact. Unfortunately, I'd come to experience just how that felt almost immediately.

Let's back up for a second. I was elated when I received the formal job offer from Salomon. I was the first student at George Mason University to graduate not only with a job on Wall Street, but also at one of the most prestigious investment banks to boot. It didn't matter that I would be the lowest-ranked person on our team—that's where you must start, right? It seemed like everything was finally panning out. That's when I got the first call from him.

I don't remember meeting John (whose name I have changed, for reasons that will become clear) during the hiring process, but I must have because I somehow became a matter of interest for him. While Salomon extended my job offer in January 1990, I wasn't due to start the training program until after I graduated. However, John started calling me after I accepted the position "just to check in." I wasn't clear what he wanted—at first it seemed like harmless, albeit confusing, chit-chat, but before long it was clear something was off. He was being far too friendly and familiar with me.

I called my girlfriends to get their take. "I'm not sure, but I think my new boss is flirting with me," I said, with a question mark in my voice. I wanted them to tell me I was wrong, but the more we discussed it, the more shaken up I became. It was not only uncomfortable, but also my nerves about starting my new job were now being multiplied by knowing I'd have to work in close proximity with him. When I started the training program in earnest, I was relieved to hear that John was traveling in Asia at the time. But the calls hardly slowed in his absence. Somehow, even with the significant time difference, he continued to badger me. While the existence of the calls alone was clearly inappropriate, the content made it even worse. He'd ask personal questions, dream about finally working down the hall from me, and talk about the dinner we must have when he returned to the States.

I knew his behavior wasn't normal, but I didn't feel I was able to decline the invitation given our status disparity. He was an executive; I was a brand-new hire. Besides, I tried to convince myself, I didn't know his intentions yet. I desperately hoped I was somehow misreading the situation, even as the alarm bells sounded. He ended up taking me to Michael's Restaurant on 55th Street, a high-end Italian bistro with wide glass walls overlooking a beautiful garden. I couldn't help but notice the way the crisply pressed tablecloths and elaborate floral arrangements on every surface screamed romance as the maître d' led us to a cozy table in the corner.

At twenty-four years old, I was just beginning to learn how to operate in the world of the wealthy and how to navigate interactions with colleagues outside of the office walls. I wasn't sure what exactly one was meant to wear on a not-date date with a man who I needed to like me a little, but not too much. I settled on a floor-length, green dress and straightened my long, curly hair down my back. In hindsight, I definitely was too formal with my apparel. John was more tastefully dressed; in fact, he oozed money. A Wharton grad with dark grayish hair, he was handsome in a refined way, even if he was slightly overweight by my midtwenties' standards.

We were hardly seated when John cut to the chase: "Everyone's going to think we're fucking, so we might as well."

I wasn't sure what to do. I let out an uncertain laugh, because I thought it was a joke at first. But no, John was serious.

"After all, we are the only single people on the team," he added.

I excused myself to go to the bathroom. I was pretty sure I was going to throw up. I counseled myself in the mirror: *You've got this, Ivy.* I had resisted advances before—what woman hasn't? I had practice handling the egos of men who weren't going to get what they wanted in a gentle enough way that we could continue being friends.

But it wasn't going to be that easy with John, and I knew it even then with my hands on either side of the bathroom sink, staring into my own reflection. I had never needed to shut down unwanted advances in a professional context with a man in a position far above mine. I tried to gather myself and headed back to the table. At the end of the meal, we got a taxi together at John's insistence. I had a pit in my stomach as we slid into the car one after the next. The door slammed shut and then, in the open backseat of an NYC cab, he tried to grope me.

I pushed him off, trying to be forceful but also respectful.

"John," I said. "I like you. But this is not a good idea. This is a new job for me, and I really need to focus on doing the best work I can."

And that was true; I needed all my wits about me for the training program which was shaping up to be more rigorous than I had anticipated. We were in class all day learning from a revolving roster of visiting professors from prestigious schools. I was intensely engaged in class discussions, always raising my hand—just like the old Ivy—especially during the accounting sessions that garnered some disapproving stares from my fellow classmates. I didn't care. If the program was going to be this competitive, I was going all in.

As I found my stride with the training, I continued to muddle my way through John's attention. At night, he would call to hear how my day went. Despite my growing repulsion at his constant attention, I tried to maintain a respectful demeanor. Could that have been perceived as me leading him on? Maybe, but I was at a loss of how else to handle the situation. The small refusals I lobbed back his way certainly didn't slow him down. After the training program ended and I started working long days and nights in the Corporate Finance Transportation group, he stepped it up a notch and absolutely overwhelmed me with his advances.

"I really like your outfit today, Ivy," he would say, slowly eying me from the ground up with his gaze coming to rest shamelessly on my chest. His glass office was several feet away from the cubicle where I sat next to Kris Kisska, a UVA graduate with whom I had become fast friends. Every time he would call me into his office, I would cringe and look at her for a reassuring nod that I was going to be okay. I had confided in her early on about this situation. My sources of female empathy were sparse as there were hardly any other women in the office.

Things continued to worsen. In the morning when I arrived at my desk and saw the blinking light on my phone indicating I had a voice-mail, my stomach would sink. I would hit playback only to hear John's voice: "Hey, I just had to tell you I really like that blouse you had on yesterday. Your cleavage looked fantastic," he'd croon in a voice I hardly recognized. Yet even as he continued leaving me explicit messages, he was somehow able to switch gears and interact with me normally and professionally in public as I performed my assignments. The way he played the two different roles so perfectly was deeply unnerving.

I hated it, but this remained the daily routine for some time—until Ross joined our team for a project, that is. Ross was only two years older than me even though he already had his MBA and was a permanent hire as an associate in the generalist pool. He was from Oklahoma and exuded a sweet gentlemanly charm made better by his also being funny and cool. He looked a little like John Denver, with longish blond hair that swooped over his forehead and brushed against eyeglasses that made him look smart and, as far as I was concerned, sexy. I had a major crush on him, and it seems that must have been pretty obvious.

John saw the chemistry between Ross and me and he was silently furious. It seemed he could tolerate my resistance to his advances, viewing it almost as a game, but it was another thing altogether for me to instead respond to a male who wasn't him. And so, John turned on me. His excessive interest gave way to an impenetrable iciness. The only times he spoke to me or acknowledged my presence were to criticize my performance. Even when I double- and triple-checked my work, but he always managed to find some minor flaw to blow way out of proportion. It was clear he had resolved to make my life hell and, just as I had done with his advances, I felt I had to grin and bear it. I put my head down and decided all I could do was try to make it through my two years in one piece.

While I was doing my best to maintain my life outside of work, I hadn't seen many of my friends in months. Maria, my former roommate, and Yvette, one of my best friends, both lived in Virginia and banded together to convince me to finally take a weekend off to come visit. On the Thursday before the trip, we pulled an all-nighter at work. I was exhausted, but I powered through knowing the long-awaited corner was only a day away. By the time John and I came down the elevator together, it was 6:00 a.m. on Friday. As the doors opened on the ground floor, he turned to me and said he'd see me back in the office later that morning.

"Okay," I said. "But don't forget that I'm going to Virginia this weekend." Seeing his expression, I hastily added, "I haven't taken a weekend off yet this year."

"Oh, that's not going to happen," he said. "You're not going anywhere, and we both know it." He let out a mean laugh.

As we walked out of 7 World Trade Center's massive glass revolving doors and went our separate directions, I had a lump in my throat. I wanted to crumble to the floor. I wanted to crawl into a hole and stay there. I wanted a break, a breather. I didn't know how I was going to survive John's abusive leadership for much longer. With a heavy heart, I canceled my trip.

My First Review

At the end of the first year of the program in June 1991, I was up for my first review. One of the directors, Pat, was the coordinator for the seventy analysts and aggregated the feedback from senior team members. He called me in for a one-on-one meeting to discuss my performance. His office was small and had glass walls, making me feel vulnerable as I settled into a chair in full view of the entire office.

Pat told me: "You have great overall ratings on your performance, with the exception of one of your direct reports."

That's all it took; everything that had been happening over the last year and a half surged out of me like a tidal wave. I started with the first phone calls I received while still at George Mason, through to the dinners and the dirty voicemails, before finally explaining how cruel John had become after I showed interest in another man. I was talking a million miles a minute. It felt good to finally unburden myself. Until Pat raised his hand to stop me.

"Ivy, it wasn't John," he said.

Oh, shit! I thought. It had not for a second occurred to me it'd be anyone else.

Pat explained that it was the new managing director, Larry, who had given me a lukewarm review at best. He had started just a few months earlier, and I had quickly decided he was insufferably pompous and was best left ignored. He often asked me to do admin work as if I were a secretary to which I'd roll my eyes and walk the stack of papers over to our actual secretary to handle, a habit he clearly resented.

When I realized I had just laid bare my biggest workplace secret over a misunderstanding, I tried to recover the situation.

"Don't do anything!" I pleaded with Pat. "It's fine now."

It really had been better as of late. John had started to settle into something between his adoration or his fury. He had even given me a decent review apparently. But Pat couldn't erase my confession.

"We are going to have to sit down with human resources," he told me.

I was nauseous at the thought of retelling the entire tale, this time to a table of HR representatives. I got that hot flash you feel when you know you've put something into motion that can't be stopped. It was as if saying it out loud was making the entire nightmare real, or letting it expand to take up more room. But at the same time, I drew comfort from the fact that I wasn't the one who set off this chain of events. While the way it came out was hardly ideal, I had given John a whole slew of opportunities to stop his behavior before it got to this point.

Shortly after the meeting with HR, I was summoned to the thirtieth floor to discuss the situation with the higher-ups. I walked into an enormous conference room where five men sat in a cluster, with Pat, the managing director of my group, as well as the head of investment banking among them. I felt panicky. I was made to tell the whole story again, now for the third time. When I had finished, the head of HR suggested I be moved out of the transportation group and put somewhere else. My nausea worsened. If I was moved, people would surely wonder why. If anybody caught wind of what had happened, I would be ridiculed. They would whisper about how the way I dressed asked for attention, or about how I brought it upon myself as a flirt or a partier. I had seen it happen before. My head was spinning, and I could barely focus on the conversation taking place around me as I worried that my career was as good as over. Finally, a question was asked of me that I didn't catch at first, so it had to be repeated.

"What do you want to do?" It was the head of investment banking speaking, an older man in an impeccably tailored suit and an Hermes tie, looking at me in a way that made it clear this was not what he wanted to have to deal with today.

All I wanted to do was make it go away.

"Look, John's backed off," I said. "Please don't move me from the transportation group. Everything's going to be fine. I promise if he causes any more trouble, I will tell you immediately." They let me stay in the Transportation Group, and I was overcome with something that felt like a less satisfying form of relief.

Walking the Line

Looking back on this experience, I'm frustrated. That was a time when women who were harassed in the workplace were almost always viewed as being at fault rather than being victims. If a woman dared to voice concern over how she was being treated, it was not support she was given but the burden of shame. However, while the system is still far from perfect, the #MeToo movement in recent years has helped change these dynamics for the better. As a society, we're still far from a system where women are heard and protected, and men are given due process when implicated in misconduct. I hope to see more progress made toward achieving that balance, but I'm nonetheless pleased every office and workplace has been put on notice there are certain behaviors that are simply unacceptable.

But the situation with John had left me wary—and that's before I realized just how gray and nuanced interacting with men in a professional context can truly be. With John, it was cut-and-dried. As a young woman in the training program, I was prey to an unfair power dynamic. I was a college student when it started, and John was a senior report. From every angle, that is unacceptable. As I got older, however, and became a full-fledged analyst on my own, I realized I needed to become savvier and more intentional with my actions, not only to protect myself from unwanted advances but also from the misinterpretation of my own behavior. When I emerged as a peer to the accomplished people in my profession, it became just as much my responsibility to know where to draw the line as it did the men with whom I was dealing.

I didn't always get it right. There were a few experiences that taught me how necessary it was to be more careful, the most significant of which occurred while I was still at Salomon. The CEO of a major, publicly traded home builder I'll call Jack was a very charismatic figure. I knew he had a bad reputation as a womanizer, even though he was twice my age and I thought of him as being old. He was already on his second wife, and he had a suspicious amount of very attractive women working in his office. I was covering his company, meaning that I wrote research on their stock and gave a recommendation as to whether those in the market should buy, hold, or sell their stock.

As an analyst, you are in a powerful position; some companies recognize that power and try to sway your position by wining and dining you as they do their best to make a convincing case for why their stock would be a great investment; that's just part of the way our business is done.

From go, Jack was one of those men who would make physical contact with me that I found uncomfortable. He'd hug me too long or grab my hand with too much intimacy. But instead of being cold to him and souring the relationship, I chose to return his friendliness in a way that I knew could be interpreted as flirting.

Throughout my teen years, I had always danced on the line separating being strategic from being manipulative. Growing up, I was willing to take risks that fortunately never ended with real trouble. I had a fake ID and could get into bars by sweet-talking the bouncers. When I was in high school, I used to pride myself on getting backstage at rock concerts by being charming and flirty. I was a smooth enough talker, I never even considered resorting to more hands-on persuasion tactics. I knew my good negotiating skills were enough to get me behind the curtain. At sixteen years old, I met Def Leppard after a concert in New Haven, Connecticut. I got backstage and met some of the band members of Motley Crew, Judas Priest, and Van Halen. My biggest coup was meeting Steven Tyler, the lead singer of Aerosmith. To my children's delight, a picture of the two of us from that night still sits on my bathroom vanity.

Now, however, I was applying those same tactics in an entirely different world. It took several misfires to realize that my willingness to take risks, to be bold and willing to do things that could result in negative consequences, needed to be tempered in the professional setting or it could turn against me. For example, I came to realize that telling stories about my wild days as a way to make people feel I was opening up to them could instead be interpreted as me signaling my willingness to do certain things to get ahead. That's what happened with Jack.

One summer, I suggested to my best friend Leisa that we take a trip to Scottsdale as I'd be able to expense most of the cost. Leisa had been a constant in my life since middle school. Although she was a single mother of three little kids, we always figured out how she could sneak away for a few days here or there to take advantage of my incredible business trips. She was my go-to partner in crime.

As a single successful professional, these boondoggles—the term we used for unnecessary, but thoroughly enjoyed work trips—were some of the best times I had in my life. The trick was figuring out a reason to be in the places you wanted to visit. For example, if I wanted to play golf at Pebble Beach, I had to set up meetings in San Francisco to warrant the trip. Because of that, I was becoming an expert at mixing business with pleasure. I knew that Jack's company had a lot of communities in the Scottsdale market, so I gave him a call and said I'd love to tour his product offering.

"Great," Jack said, "I'll meet you there."

I stumbled over my words. "Wow, you don't have to come all the way out here. Just set me up with one of your guys who runs it."

"Oh, no, I insist," he responded. "I need to go there anyway!"

Being shown around his business in Scottsdale somehow gave way to Leisa and I sharing a cozy dinner with Jack. He took us to a very expensive restaurant set inside an Art Deco–style hotel with stunning views of an orchid-filled courtyard. It was clear Jack was well-known by everyone who worked there and many of the diners as well. His charm was on full display, as was his command of the wine list. When we got up from the table, Jack casually invited us to his room for a nightcap. After his generosity, we felt we could hardly refuse such a simple request. But it was moments after settling onto his suite's couch that Leisa and I began catching each other's eyes, realizing we had gone a step too far by agreeing to be there. It was becoming increasingly clear Jack assumed we were going to top the night off with some intimacy.

We didn't, of course. We got out of there before he could even get us a drink. Now, Jack was undoubtedly being inappropriate, trying to take advantage of women half his age. We were in our twenties and he was in his forties. But we certainly didn't mind his attention when it meant a free dinner at an expensive and exclusive restaurant. We knew he was being flirtatious but, as we had grown accustomed to doing in our rebellious teen years, we thought we could play our cards right to get what we wanted out of the bargain. Looking back, it was naive to think he wouldn't be expecting anything in return and foolish to have contributed to the flirtation, even in what had felt like a strategic and controlled way.

I want to make clear that it wasn't okay for him to expect anything in return for his kindness, and I'm also not saying you can't be friendly to your colleagues. I'm saying don't think you are cleverer than you are. Don't try to manipulate people when your high-quality work should be enough. I learned a valuable lesson that night. I had to take responsibility for how my actions had contributed to the stressful and unsavory situation I found myself in and think about what I would do differently next time around. I vowed to make a better effort to separate my entertainment from my career.

Chapter Three

CREATE YOUR OWN RESOURCES
(AND DON'T BE AFRAID TO BUG PEOPLE)

"So, Ivy, what drives you: Power, prestige, or money?"

Before landing my spot in the training program at Salomon Brothers, I heard repeatedly about those "Ivy League kids." It was made clear immediately and continually that Wall Street hired students only from the most prestigious schools. I'm sure I don't need to tell you that no firm ever came to George Mason to recruit. Even before I officially joined the industry, I was made painfully aware of the strong hierarchy between educational institutions in the eyes of human resources and the ultimate decision-makers. I hoped that the qualities of perseverance and resilience would outweigh something as simple as the name on my diploma, but it was so deflating that there was a small pool of applicants valued so much more highly than everyone else based on name recognition alone.

When I wiggled my way into Salomon Brothers despite my lack of Ivy League education, I hoped having a job on Wall Street would be an equalizer, that where I obtained my education would matter less and less as my experience grew. But when I got to the end of my two-year training program, that elitism raised its ugly head again. From the moment I accepted the role, I knew that the clock was ticking on my time at Salomon; by design, my position would be gone by the middle of 1992. Nearly everybody from the program was applying to MBA programs at the top schools. The widely accepted sentiment was that if you didn't go to a Harvard, Stanford, or Wharton, your graduate degree was worth shit. I heard it from the others in my program, and I heard it from the higher-ups. I was shocked. It was as if the two years spent working for a leading investment bank on Wall Street meant nothing, like they had never happened. I was starting to feel like I'd forever be handicapped by not boasting an educational brand name.

I felt pressured to follow the lead of the people around me. Many of them had come from the world I had so newly joined, and it seemed foolish to ignore the opinions they put forward as fact. I applied to three business schools: Harvard, Stanford, and Northwestern. I put everything I had into the process. I spent hours on the applications, hired a tutor to help me write the essays, and studied for the GMATs for weeks, taking practice test after practice test. It was a massive commitment, but I was driven by a single thought; if I didn't get into a top school, I would be labeled a failure. In hindsight, the only one likely to do so would have been myself, but I had grown used to assuming a defensive position because of my background. I felt I was still in a fight to survive.

Even with knowing how selective all three institutions were, I felt optimistic about my chances of getting in. My undergraduate GPA had been high, yes, but I also figured the fact that I had financed my own education by working full-time through school paired with my two years of working experience at Salomon would give me a real leg up. Combined with the effort I had put into my application; I was feeling good. Then, all three schools rejected me. I was shocked at first, then shattered, before deciding I was mostly just angry. I momentarily considered applying to a business school that wasn't in the top tier, but I couldn't help but dwell on how expensive MBA programs were, even back then. I asked myself: "Do I really want to take on more student loans?" The answer was a resounding no. If I was going to put myself further in the hole, it had to be for something extraordinary. I reminded myself that the untraditional Ivy approach had gotten me onto Wall Street despite the odds, and so I decided to silence the opinions swirling around me and continue to trust my instincts. I resolved to do the best I could with my undergraduate degree.

Power, Prestige, or Money

Fortunately for me, the end of my two-year program coincided with a scandal at Salomon Brothers. In late 1991, the firm was experiencing a major backlash from the treasury scandal which saw CEO John Gutfreund resign, causing many of the best professionals in the company to jump ship as they worried Salomon was about to go under. While those higher up were deeply rattled, I welcomed the turnover and turmoil from my very junior role. The economy had been mired in a housing-led recession that dragged the whole economy down, and there weren't a lot of jobs available on the open market. But because of the internal drama, Salomon happened to have more opportunities than normal at the time I was looking. I'd take my wins where I could find them.

I underwent a series of internal interviews before accepting the first role I was offered. I relied on the support and knowledge of my mentors heavily in the beginning. One such mentor was Julius Maldutis, a tall, middle-aged man with gray hair and thick glasses whose smile lit up the room. Julius was a highly ranked, tenured airline analyst who taught me a lot about analyzing companies during my two years working in the transportation group. He was always available to support me when I needed his input on pitches, or to help me understand specifics about the airline industry. I felt fortunate that he had my back, and we quickly became great friends. It was Julius who eventually recommended I apply for an associate job opening in the equity research department where I'd be working under a senior equity analyst named Bruce Harting.

At the time, Bruce followed the Savings and Loan industry—alive and well in those days—and the Government Sponsored Entities (GSEs), Freddie Mac and Fannie Mae, which were still public companies at the time. Because Bruce knew so much about the mortgage industry given his coverage universe, he had agreed to pick up the housing stocks as a favor to the firm. Julius assured me that I would be perfect for the job and promised to put in a good word for me.

Julius's confidence in the role shift being good for me was matched, perhaps even outstripped, by everyone else thinking it'd be the worst choice I could make. The investment bankers on my team, along with anyone else I asked, were totally against the idea of my going to work in equity research. They justified their stance by saying that equity analysts were monkeys simply repeating what public company management teams told them to say. This was a time when investment bankers ruled Wall Street, although this would change later; their arrogance was palpable, and I wasn't sure how much that factored into what they were telling me. But I didn't feel like I was able to be picky and so with Julius's recommendation, Bruce decided to consider me for the position.

The first of many interviews was with George Shapiro, a tenured managing director who helped with recruiting talent as well as being the #1 ranked aerospace analyst. The meeting was informal and took place in the cafeteria at lunch. It started off slow, with little more than small talk. Then, he abruptly pivoted and began firing questions at me.

"So, Ivy, what drives you: Power, prestige, or money?" He asked.

He must have seen the alarm on my face as he assured me there wasn't a right answer. He just wanted to get a sense of where I was coming from.

I took a deep breath and said, "Prestige."

He looked at me.

"If I earn prestige, then I'm going to have money and money is a big part of what makes someone powerful."

He must have appreciated that response because I was moved forward. I tackled the interview process with intentionality. Many of the traits I had developed over the past several years were put to good use: I was inquisitive, ambitious, and took my preinterview research seriously so I could make the most of each interaction with the team and come across as knowledgeable and competent, all while maintaining a humble and eager demeanor. Each interview went as well as the last as I met with representatives of the research and sales teams. As the process ended, I was delighted to be offered the position.

I learned quickly that Bruce was a hands-off manager who gave his team total autonomy. While I welcomed that approach later in my career, I was alarmed to be left to my own devices. I didn't know what I was doing, and it seemed clear that Bruce didn't have much time to teach me. I'd hover around his door, waiting for a break between his meetings or his phone calls to pop inside for a quick check-in. Bruce would look up at me with his thick glasses and slicked back hair and ask, "What's up?"

I'd fire off a string of rapid questions, looking for clarification and, as always since my Arthur Young days, looking for more work to do.

I'm sure I was annoying him to no end, but I was in the deep end without a life jacket. Even though I was unclear on exactly what I was meant to be doing, I was publishing notes and changing estimates. I was way beyond the tips of my skis, as the expression goes, and relied on other associates to teach me as I pounded them with endless questions.

After a few months of my well-intentioned but uninformed zeal, it was decided I should go through the firm's MBA training program, famously depicted in Michael Lewis's book, *Liar's Poker*. It would speed up my learning curve and provide me with a stronger foundation to be successful. When the eight-week course came to an end, I would be given a full year to analyze the housing industry before I would then be expected to launch coverage on the stocks. Salomon wanted to see what I was capable of once I had been properly equipped.

As my second in-house training program commenced, I quickly realized what an incredible opportunity it was. There were over one hundred trainees, including six others like me who had already been placed in a sector and, therefore, didn't have to rotate through the various areas of the firm like everyone else in the program. I also realized I was the sole trainee without an MBA; I knew I was extremely fortunate to be able to participate and vowed I would do anything to succeed.

I remember the summer of 1992 spent in the MBA training program as one of the hardest, yet most rewarding, periods of my career. It had been far easier to stand out in the two-year training program I had earlier completed. Then, my accounting background instilled me with confidence as a portion of the other trainees didn't have a clue about finance; we called them the "poets"—English or history majors Salomon hired to flesh out the team with people who knew how to write and how to think differently than those who were numbers-oriented.

There were no poets in the MBA training program. Everyone came from an accounting or finance background, boasting master's degrees from the best business schools in the country. We were studying advanced topics in bond math, such as convexity, the nonlinear relationship bond prices respond to changes in interest rates, and derivatives and currencies, all of which I knew nothing about. Our classes were highly competitive with intensive assignments and a steady stream of exams to assess our progress. Despite the intimidating environment, my willingness to raise my hand and annoy those around me in the pursuit of getting my questions answered persisted. Yet I couldn't help but feel I was perpetually playing catch-up with what other people seemed to have already learned.

In true nineties Wall Street fashion, Salomon made sure to dazzle us trainees with the good life to remind us why it was worth undertaking such a rigorous course and choosing them as our employer. The competition to lure in the best of the best was fierce on "The Street." On a near nightly basis, Salomon would put on elaborate events to entertain us, renting out entire restaurants with live music, hosting scavenger hunts and softball games, even arranging a casino night on a massive yacht. And no matter what the plan was, we could count on an unbelievable spread of food and alcohol. It was important to the firm that we bond as a team and, more importantly, that we were convinced Salomon was the greatest place to work under the sun. That's how Wall Street operated in those days; the unspoken contract was that constant wining and dining equaled employee loyalty and longevity.

It was on one of these nights that I met Laura, who worked in high yield and was my age. We bonded immediately and were inseparable from that point forward. She became my north star and served as my sounding board day and night. I couldn't have fully understood it then, but I would need every shred of help I could get.

I genuinely believe that enrolling in the MBA training program was crucial to my future success. One of the realities of working on Wall Street is that people don't have time to teach you your role, and yet you're expected to do it, and to do it well. In those days, there was no internet to help research what was expected of you. Instead, you had to be persistent and create your own resources; before the program, this basically meant I had to bug people relentlessly until they decided to spare me a few minutes. By contrast, an eight-week intensive course felt like luxury even while being so mentally draining.

Trust Takes Time

Every firm on Wall Street holds a morning call. Picture a large room just off the trading floor filled with salespeople. It's 7:15 a.m.—not an hour when people tend to be at their best, but the earliness is necessary; there is much information that needs to be exchanged and business transacted before the market opens at 9:30 a.m. And so, we would gather. For those unable to be physically present, there was a transmission system that allowed sales traders, salespeople, and Salomon professionals spread across the world to listen in.

The product manager who ran the calls was responsible for deciding which analysts would be speaking each morning and in what order they'd present. There could be ten or even twenty analysts on one call, based on ratings or earnings changes in our respective sectors, or a specific event or meeting one of us had hosted that it seemed pertinent to share.

Whenever it was my turn to present, I reminded myself to speak slowly and clearly and, most important, to sound confident.

After an analyst finished speaking, salespeople were given the floor to question the call. It wasn't unusual for it to get somewhat confrontational. "How can you upgrade that stock now when interest rates are rising? Do you really want us to tell clients to buy it here?"

The intensity of salespeople's responses was sometimes warranted, but often not. Most were concerned with sounding smart as they knew the senior heads were listening in. But a bad call from an analyst truly could make a salesperson look bad in front of their clients, which could create bad blood and lead to reduction in their compensation. As an analyst speaking on the morning call, it was important not to appear nervous as that would almost surely lead to a feeding frenzy of negativity. While good salespeople ask tough questions, I saw analysts reduced to tears being dressed down in public on more than one occasion.

To help combat my nerves, I would prepare as thoroughly as possible before I went on a morning call. Laura was an invaluable part of that process. She would get to the office at 6:00 a.m. for her job in high yield which meant that if I came in earlier as well, I could sit at her desk on the trading floor and practice with her. She was willing to listen to me practice over and over again, giving feedback and helping me fine-tune my word choices. The process was nerve-racking, all the way down to the walk to the morning call room itself, which saw me hoof it across the entire length of the football-field-sized trading floor at 7 World Trade. In fact, it was the largest trading floor on Wall Street aside from the New York Stock Exchange itself. The route to the door had blocks of desks on either side. It was almost as if it had been constructed to make you feel as exposed and vulnerable as possible. When I passed Laura's desk, I'd look at her for final reassurance. Here I go, I would mouth. She would smile and I would take a final deep breath.

I thought I did a fair job hiding how nervous I was, but my neck proved otherwise. I didn't think it was noticeable, but I broke out in a rash nearly every time I presented on the morning call in those early years. Every time I walked out of the call room; I'd see a guy sitting in the corner in a low-riding swivel chair on the perched platform all the salespeople sat on with a cocky smirk on his face. It was David Zelman, one of Salomon's best salespeople and someone positively oozing with confidence. One day, he waved me over.

"Hey, good morning! Why is your neck so red?" he said.

I flushed even more deeply. "It is not!" I was mortified he would call me out on it, and all while laughing quietly to himself. I stalked away, wholly unaware this man would soon become my mentor and, eventually, my husband.

I'm not sure if he was flirting or simply trying to be a supportive colleague in those early days, but David became a source of professional wisdom for me. Taking full advantage of his knowledge and friendliness, I besieged him with questions so I could excel as an analyst. He was happy to help informally, but then something serendipitous happened. The heads of research and sales decided to try a new system in which each new analyst was assigned a salesperson to show them the ropes. David was officially assigned to me, and I was thrilled; he was something of a rock star at the firm, covering some of the biggest accounts in his territory of Philadelphia. But beyond that, he was set apart by his business approach; he didn't follow the normal protocols and he was never political. He instead made the calls that he thought were good investment ideas, acting as an effective buffer for his clients who he sincerely cared about.

David helped me understand what salespeople appreciated, and how best to articulate my recommendations. He told me that it would take time for the sales force to trust my calls and I had to be patient. That was hard for me. I wanted to be a star and outperform everyone's expectations, but when I went on the morning call, I was talking about housing stuff that very few people cared about. On a good day, no more than 10 percent of the salespeople would be actively listening to what I had to say. Which was fair enough; my stocks represented less than 1 percent of the S&P 500. Back in those years, when someone from Ford or GE got on the call, by contrast, everyone was all ears. Yet despite this context, I couldn't help but feel it was the most important thing in the whole world when my turn came.

David was an amazing teacher. Once he realized I was passionate and determined, he was willing to help however he could. That's true of most good mentors; they're willing to give more of their time when their mentee is eager and hungry to succeed. I soaked up everything he taught me—typing like wildfire as he lectured. I'd always holler at him to slow down which only made him laugh. He got a kick out of me; he knew I wouldn't stop pestering until he answered all my questions. I believe that a mentee who wants to be successful must be persistent. I tell that to the students who come to me today for advice about their career development: I'm not going to chase you down. You have to chase me down. Show me you care.

An Equity Sell Side Analyst

David helped build my confidence and as I got more comfortable in my role, my passion for it grew. The job of an equity sell side analyst is extremely diverse, but their primary role is to become an expert on the industry they're assigned to. Analysts are expected to get down to the nuts and bolts of it: the size of the industry, the competitive landscape, industry growth rates, cost inputs, historical performance and drivers for demand. The next step is to study the specific companies in the sector by digging into their history and analyzing their performance to determine if they would be good investments. I'd ask myself questions like, *Have they delivered strong returns to shareholders? Is their strategy compelling? Is their performance consistent? What's their point of differentiation?* I'd meet with leadership at the company I was researching, and then go meet with their competitors to compare and contrast their business models. It takes that level of intense immersion in the space for a sell side analyst to be truly equipped to make a recommendation to institutional investors on whether they should buy, sell, or hold the stock.

It's a balancing act to maintain ongoing research on an industry, company visits, calls and meetings with clients, and conferences in a variety of states. We'd publish research on our sectors, listen to calls, and update their earnings models before reporting back to the sales force on any changes to their estimates or views on their stocks. It was never boring, rather I found the work electrifying. Every day brought something new.

One of the most important pieces of advice David gave me was not to simply parrot what I was told by the management teams of the companies I covered. Whether a salesperson or an analyst, it's necessary to ask hard questions and do additional digging of your own. While there were people at Salomon who did listen to and accept whatever the executive teams told them, the top performers took a more objective, independent approach.

To this end, David recommended I channel check. This meant identifying private companies or suppliers in the public company's ecosystem that were willing to share their informed industry perspective with me.

The private firms provided me a thorough education on the sector which helped me distill the right questions to ask the public companies I covered, questions I'm sure they wished I didn't ask. Not depending on the packaged message given by public companies' management teams was a rule David drilled into me that would become one of the primary building blocks for my dominance in the housing industry in years to come.

It turns out I was good at asking the right questions of the right people. I quickly gained a reputation as being an analyst asking the tough, but important questions. Various members of management would later go on to tell me they hated it when it was my turn to ask a question on the conference calls. I would relentlessly probe topics they were not comfortable elaborating on and was willing to call them out when it seemed they were not being forthcoming.

A shift was taking place. At the beginning of my career in investment banking, I'd silently hover on the edges of meeting rooms, feeling lucky to be allowed to even attend. Now, I was visiting publicly-traded companies as an analyst and regularly found myself in meetings where it was just the CEO, the CFO, the head of investor relations, and myself around a small table. Gone were the days of me fighting for a blip of airtime or a shred of recognition; now, these executives were the ones trying to win me over, telling me their strategy and providing an in-depth overview of their business they needed me to believe in. I was also at Salomon, a firm The Street took seriously. The reversal of power was exhilarating.

While I relished being taken more seriously, my humble past was never far from my mind and proved to be a valuable point of difference that set me apart from other analysts. Even as I gained the respect of my peers, I was willing to admit there were things I didn't know, and I remained hungry to learn from everyone I came across. I would ask management teams and even clients to share their views on how I could cover the sector more effectively, which was an unusual approach: What do you think I should be focused on? What are other analysts not writing about in the housing sector that you think is worthwhile? What's missing in the current analysis? I felt like a detective, constantly asking questions, collecting data, and piecing things together to form a whole and thoroughly corroborated story.

As I began to travel more for work, my professional network ballooned. One of my first trips was to visit the Joint Center for Housing at Harvard University, an industry association. The director, Jim Brown, was moved by my passion for the sector and was eager to help me however he could. He was the one to introduce me to my first private homebuilder, Larry Webb, the CEO of John Laing Homes based in Newport Beach, California. From New York originally, Larry was the most down to earth professional I had met thus far; he was a sports fanatic and had previously taught high school history. We bonded immediately. He took me under his wing and showed me the ropes.

I quickly ended up with a roster of a few dozen private builders I had met at industry conferences or through referrals who I would call monthly to discuss their operating trends: sales performance, pricing power, land availability, and so forth. They enjoyed talking about their business and appreciated my thirst to learn. My contact book swelled further as the builders began introducing me to their suppliers. My first strong supplier contact was Rich Maresco, a kitchen and bath distributor from my old stomping grounds in Northern Virginia. Rich educated me on the cabinet industry which I ended up needing to understand to cover Masco, a leading building products manufacturer in my coverage universe. It was becoming clear how interconnected the industry was, and how important it was not to underestimate a single contact.

The importance of establishing and maintaining contacts has stayed with me throughout my career. Professionally, I have grown up with many of the contacts I made in my earliest days at Salomon. While I knew I still had to understand historical housing metrics and how they correlated to one another by performing statistical regression analyses and building complex models, I had a gut for the business. Modeling was standard procedure, uniform and unremarkable. It was the people you knew that made the difference. I constantly met new contacts through old ones and my Rolodex exploded. Their proprietary insight gave me a real edge against my competitors.

I have never lost my delight of learning from people who I respect. To this day, I tend to pepper everybody I meet with questions. I want to hear their story. *Where did you grow up? What school did you go to? How did you get started in your career?* I'm genuinely curious, and I believe that natural curiosity is crucial to becoming a successful analyst. Arrogance won't get you anywhere. A desire to learn, a willingness to be open-minded and accept information that challenges your current beliefs, and the humility to acknowledge you don't know everything will take you far in the business world, regardless of what industry you're in.

Then and now, mining for new insights and discovering information that reshapes my analysis keeps my competitive juices flowing. And it proved to be that very emphasis on industry networking that became the foundation for my future success.

1. Caryn at the top, cousin Janet left, Ally and Ivy (1973)

2. Sprinkle, Ivy, Cinnamon and Ally (1980)

3. Yvette and Ivy in London—9th grade (1981)

4. Yvette and Ivy in Switzerland (1981)

5. Ivy, Leisa with some crazy unknown man (1984)

6. Ian and Ivy (1986)

7. Maria and Ivy (1989)

8. Arthur Young secretaries, including Maria (1989)

9. Ivy and Dad (1984)

10. Ivy and Ally (1988)

11. Ivy and Steven Tyler (1988)

12. Ivy (1990)

13. Ivy in front of WTC (1990)

14. Maria, Ally, Ivy and Mom (1988)

15. Grandma Ruthe, Ivy and David (1998)

16. Malinda and Ivy in front of 7 WTC (1995)

17. Malinda and Ivy at my wedding (1998)

18. My Dad and Maryann at my wedding (1998)

19. Ivy and David (1997)

20. Maria, Yvette, Jennifer, Doreen, Elena and Amanda (1998)

21. Ivy and Laura skiing in Vail (1994)

22. Leisa, Ivy, Laura and Yvette in London (1993)

23. Ivy and Zoey in Rosemary Beach (2000)

24. Moe (2021)

25. Zia, Zoey and Zach (2004)

26. Ivy, Zoey, Malinda and my Dad in Rosemary Beach (2005)

27. Ivy, Zach, Zia and Zoey (2011)

28. Zoey at dance competition (2010)

29. Zia and Zilli (2009)

30. Ivy and Jody at David's 40th Birthday (2002)

31. Ivy and Doreen (2002)

32. Ivy and Zach in Anguilla (2014)

Chapter Four

SMILE AND DIAL
(GOD GAVE YOU TWO EARS AND ONE MOUTH FOR A REASON)

*"Hi, we've never spoken before.
How long have you been with the company?"*

When I officially launched on my sector at Salomon in August of 1993, I immediately started calling clients to introduce myself. In the office it was known as "smiling and dialing." Many of Salomon's clients had a professional who was responsible for covering housing stocks and I was determined to build a relationship with every one of them. I was fed off the competitive energy simmering among the analysts for motivation. We were each starving for recognition and doing all we could to be the best in our respective sectors. So, we pounded the phones and tried to be the one to call the most clients in a day. If you went to voicemail, you left a message, and then moved right along to the next person on the list.

When I started covering the housing sector, there wasn't a lot of interest in my space given the negligible weighting my stocks had in the

S&P 500. Additionally, I launched on just four homebuilding stocks at first—Centex, Hovnanian, Pulte Homes, and KB Homes—so even keeping a conversation going proved to be a challenge. The silver lining of being in a relatively overlooked sector was that it pushed me to rely on building personal connections with clients to make sure they welcomed my call.

My goal wasn't to impress the person on the other end of the line with what I knew about the housing industry or launch into a long pitch about a stock. Instead, I put the focus on what they were thinking. The calls that were the most valuable to me were the ones in which I hardly spoke. Whether they were going on about their sector views, their career journey, or their personal lives, I wanted to get them talking. I wanted them to feel like I was the student, and they were the teacher—because, really, they were. As my father-in-law likes to say, God gave you two ears and one mouth for a reason.

Of course, I did pipe up here and there with what I thought would be valuable and appreciated insights which would help ensure whoever was on the other end of the line wanted to take my call the next time I rang. The goal was to get my contacts to a place where they looked forward to hearing, "Ivy Schneider is on the phone . . ."

Winning clients over and becoming their go-to analyst would, in turn, boost my reputation inside the firm. If clients mentioned me by name to their salesperson, that salesperson would then be more compelled to pay attention to what I was saying about my space. More support externally and internally translated into greater prestige and then, of course, higher compensation. Sound familiar? Prestige first, then money, and finally power.

Something that many people overlook, in business and in life, is balancing their interactions with others. It's good to pause and ask yourself: *Are we both sharing? Does this feel mutual? Or is it one-sided?* Getting people to open up about themselves, their lives, and their sector perspectives not only served to make them feel good, but also established trust. By making clear the conversation was not just about me, but us, it was easier for the client to feel confident our professional relationship would be mutually beneficial as well.

Recently I asked a mentee of mine who was working as a junior accountant at a good-sized firm of around two hundred people: "How many of the people there who inspire you, or seem interesting to you, have you spoken to?"

"Oh, I haven't talked to anybody," she said in a rush.

I was incredulous. "Why not?"

"I don't want to bother them."

We too often forget that people love to share their stories, especially when they feel like they're being helpful. If you get someone to share their story with you, they're naturally going to start being more interested in you in return and will admire your determination rather than be put off by your enthusiasm.

It's never too early to begin developing this skill. If you're still in school, ask your favorite professor about their career path. Truly listen to what they have to say, without interrupting or shifting the focus back to yourself. It might feel hard or awkward the first few times, but the fear quickly diminishes as you realize the value of the advice and assistance being so willingly shared with you.

People Have Birthdays (and You Should Know Them)

As important as it is to listen, it is equally necessary to remember. Whatever rapport you build in a first conversation is dashed in a second when it becomes clear you hardly remember a word they said. Whenever I talked to someone new, I would take notes. *Are they married? How many children do they have? How old are they? What do they like to do outside of work? When is their birthday?*

I would listen for personal connections that could organically draw us together. Toward the start of my career, that might've been a shared love of the same sport or team. For example, I found out a company CFO I worked with was a big Wisconsin Badgers fan. I can talk college football all day long thanks to growing up with a sports maniac father and being married to a football nut. It infused our conversations with liveliness and playful competition. Now, these connections often gravitate around my children. If someone says they have kids, I'll ask their ages to see if we have overlap. If they're in the same age range, we can commiserate about the parenting challenges we're facing and share in the victories. If they are older, I always ask, "Are they still on the payroll?" If their kids are younger than mine, I can still relate. "Oh my God, I remember those days. It can be rough, huh?"

I welcomed when conversations spun off in an unexpected direction. By staying flexible rather than being overly rigid about what I planned to discuss, I was able to pick up valuable, peripheral insights that sometimes prompted me to pursue entirely different lines of questioning than I would have done otherwise. Listening for new concepts or watching unexpected trends develop over a day of calls created carry-on opportunities to boot. I'd jump off one interesting conversation before dialing up another trusted contact to ask him or her to speak to the new pattern that seemed to be taking shape.

I also came to learn that simple gestures make big impacts. Something as easy as a birthday wish can go a long way with a professional contact. It would take thirty seconds to jot the date down in my calendar and reach out briefly when the day rolled around. And yet, whether a junior analyst or a CEO, people want to be treated kindly and feel that they're valued as a person.

Once I cold-called a C-Suite executive at a major building products company located in Dalton, Georgia, as part of my proactive outreach to add industry executives to my network. From go, it was clear we couldn't be more different. He had a thick southern drawl and worked in a small town. I sported a slight New York accent and worked in the heart of the

Big Apple. But I was humble and courteous, and the executive agreed to give me a few minutes to hear what I had to say.

"I'm hoping you might be interested in receiving my housing research in exchange for your input on what's going on in the flooring business," I explained.

"Uh, yeah, I guess I am," he said, sounding distracted.

"Great. First, Ken, I'd love to hear about you and your company. How long have you been at Shaw?"

Even in the silence before he began speaking, the shift in energy was palpable. The executive launched into a fifteen-minute account of his life and his time at the company. He seemed surprised by my sincere interest in what he was saying and he was happy to share. With one call, I cemented a relationship that would last for decades. Furthermore, Ken went on to introduce me to Jim Gould, the CEO of one of the largest flooring distributors in the country, who has since been like a grandfather to my children. Jim never forgets to wish my three children happy birthday and of course showers me with love on my own birthday. After Jim believed in me, he then introduced me to all of the other major distributors in the U.S., giving me a firm grasp of what was happening in the sector. This allowed me to make key market moving calls while the whole time having my network to reinforce my views.

When I launched my own firm years later, I knew our business model had to prioritize and protect these integral human connections even as new technology meant we could rely on automation and opt never to talk to anyone again if we so chose. That was simply not an option. Our analysts regularly reach out to industry executives. I cannot deny that our automated platform has become necessary as our network of nearly one thousand business owners and operators has grown too large to call everyone on a regular basis. Still, I have made sure that reaching out by phone is a part of my team's daily routine, and I believe these conversations are the backbone of our firm.

While we provide research to the companies in our network in return for their perspective, many go above and beyond with the insight they provide us. Take Bert Selva, for example, the president and CEO of Shea Homes, one of the largest privately held homebuilders in America. Bert's support over the past few decades has been invaluable; with his scale matching many publicly traded companies, his knowledge and experience has been crucial to our understanding of public homebuilders' operations. By this point, we have grown to be good friends and I've done my best to make sure he knows how much I appreciate his time and efforts. Being so generously invested in by executives like Bert makes me crave to pay it forward in turn.

The Networking Never Ends

It isn't just the people at the top who you have to connect with. Because of my own experience as an administrative assistant at Arthur Young, I have always fostered a deep respect for people in supporting roles. I remember how surprised and delighted I was during that phase of my life when someone higher up showed genuine interest in me. Once I shifted to the other side of that relationship, I knew I needed to place as much importance on getting to know admins as I did on building relationships with executives. If I had a 2:00 p.m. call scheduled, for example, I'd call over fifteen minutes earlier to catch up with the secretary, asking about his or her weekend, family, and if they had any exciting plans coming up.

There are also business benefits to making this one of your priorities. When shit hits the fan and I need a certain CEO to speak with me immediately, regardless of whatever lunch or meeting he or she was in the middle of, my relationship with a secretary is invaluable. Being a known and liked person in the mind of the gatekeeper can make all the difference to being patched through to an executive as a priority.

Much of building a network boils down to remembering that everyone you interact with, at any level, is a human being. There is nothing to be gained from panicking or being curt, and everything to be gained from exuding positivity. A situation arose recently where I needed insight from a massive mortgage entity, and I needed it fast. My usual contact who runs the division was out of the office and I ended up on the phone with someone I had never spoken to before. Rather than beat this person over the head with my credentials or convince her my need was urgent, I took a deep breath and put a smile into my voice. "Hi, we've never spoken before. How long have you been with the company?"

The answer was thirty-seven years.

"Thirty-seven years? No way! That's almost unheard-of these days," I said. "I'll bet you've seen a lot of changes in the industry over that time . . ."

She laughed, and we settled into a conversation. Ten minutes later and wouldn't you know it? The person I had originally called to speak to just so happened to become available. I thanked my new phone friend for the time and told her I looked forward to speaking to her again, and then I was off to the races.

Some of my greatest teachers over the years have been the CEOs of publicly traded companies. While I was not dependent on them for my analysis, it would be wrong not to acknowledge their years of patient schooling on the market which had a significant impact on my career path. Many individuals played important roles in my nearly thirty-year career, but three bear mention, beginning with Robert Strudler.

Bob was chairman and CEO of US Home, a publicly traded company that was eventually acquired by Lennar, where he became COO. Bob was dedicated to his company, his family, and many philanthropic causes. He taught me the importance of building a company's culture and warned me that the greatest risk in homebuilding was failing to grow management in tandem with the market—words of wisdom I made sure to share with my all my associates who I have developed throughout my career.

My second notable mentor was Chris Connor, the former chairman and CEO of Sherwin Williams. After working his way up in the company for sixteen years, Chris became CEO at the turn of the millennium. He had big shoes to fill given that Jack Breen, the former CEO, was a legend. Chris more than delivered; he was the most charismatic and dynamic leader I had ever met, and he soon earned himself the reputation as being the greatest CEO in the S&P 500. Chris was warm and thoughtful but could be hard-hitting when necessary. Under his leadership, the company generated consistent double-digit growth with superior returns on equity. But, more important as far as I was concerned, Chris made everyone around him feel special as he took a genuine interest in people's lives. When we met for the occasional lunch, he never failed to ask about my family or compliment me on our firm's research. He gave wise and compassionate advice and truly cared about his thousands of employees. At my firm's annual housing summit, Chris would get on stage and delight the audience by announcing Sherwin's color of the year, never failing to get the crowd laughing with his great sense of humor. John Morikis, his successor, has continued this tradition.

The third leader in the home building industry who helped fundamentally shape my career is Stuart Miller, the chairman of the board of Lennar. Stuart is unlike anyone else I have ever met. He's a brilliant man who thrives on solving the impossible. When we met nearly twenty-five years ago, soon after he became the CEO of Lennar, I was intimidated by his intensity. But over time, I came to value his input to the point that he became the first person I seek out during difficult times. He is a tireless, thoughtful leader who is always willing to help others, from donating time and money to numerous charities to spending time with his grandchildren. From a business perspective, the kite never flies high enough for Stuart as he seeks to innovate the homebuilding industry and push his people to be the best they can be. Additionally, he has always ensured that Lennar is an open book. Whereas most analysts are only able to meet with the CEO, the CFO, and the investor relations person, Stuart allowed me to reach out to division or regional presidents and anyone else I thought could help me better understand the inner workings of Lennar's business.

While these three men have been mainstays in my life over the span of decades, the networking never ends. To this day, I am adding new and meaningful contacts to my network. It doesn't just stop one day when you've "made it." If you want to be as successful as you possibly can, you need to embrace networking as a way of life.

An example of a newer, but equally treasured, addition to my roster is Howard W. "Hoby" Hanna IV. Hoby is president of Howard Hanna, the third-largest real estate company in the nation who happens to live in Cleveland. When our firm decided we needed to build a real estate broker survey after several companies went public in that space, the first thing I did was ask my existing contacts if they knew any of the top brokers or owner executives that they could introduce me to. Just like that, Rei Mesa, an executive with WCI Communities, connected me with Hoby.

Hoby and I bonded immediately, and he went out of his way to give us a thorough education on the space; he introduced us to a significant number of other independent brokers, connected us with other leading firms, and provided us with fantastic testimonials as to why people would value our research—a crucial component as we were starting from scratch. Hoby played such an instrumental role in the new area of our business that I genuinely don't know if I would have been able to accomplish what I set out to do without him as an anchor. Maybe I would have eventually made headway, but it would certainly have taken much longer.

Hoby and I regularly have breakfast at a nearby pancake house. Our connection is more than just business. Sure, we discuss industry trends, but we also catch up on family updates, how our kids are doing at school, and any recent milestones we've celebrated in our respective homes. That kind of relationship, one that is built on friendship, is what makes the business world go round.

Chapter Five

GO UP AGAINST A BUFFETT

(IF YOU HAVE TO)

"Mike, what the fuck?"

Perhaps no single story better illustrates the doors opened by building relationships than the time I needed to speak to my contact, Mike Rozen, a handsome and charismatic man who was just a few years older than me. I had become genuine friends with his secretary, Ruth, over the years. Whenever I called Mike, Ruth and I would chat for ages before she transferred me, asking after one another's children by name or sometimes just discussing a good movie that had just come out. Ruth knew me well enough to hear the panic in my voice the second she picked up the phone.

"Ivy, breathe. It's going to be okay. I'll find him," she said.

Finally, I heard, "Hold for Mike Rozen."

I let out a deep breath I didn't realize I was holding. I desperately needed this conversation to happen. I knew Mike's input would help me to stay strong at a pivotal point in a call I had to make on a stock.

I need to back up. After blazing a path at Salomon Brothers and earning the respect of my peers both internally and externally, I was abruptly let go. It was a matter of logistics rather than an issue with my performance, but I was upset, nonetheless. There was an annual poll published by *Institutional Investor* magazine that ranked which analysts were the most valued by investors in their respective sectors; it was a massive deal within the industry, like the Academy Awards for analysts. If you nabbed a spot in the top three, you became an overnight success. By 1997, I found myself ranked #2. However, in that same year, Smith Barney acquired Salomon Brothers and brought their own housing analyst along with them, Dave Dwyer. Dave, as fate would have it, was ranked #1. They had no need for both of us, and it was obvious who'd get the boot. When the details of the rankings were published months later, we'd come to find out Dave had only been ten basis points ahead of me, yet the narrow loss was still enough to send my career off in a new trajectory. Toward the end of that year, I packed up my things and moved to the Gramercy Park area, setting up shop as the housing analyst at Credit Suisse with my associate Ian Lapey at my side.

Given my propensity toward loyalty, I would have most likely been a lifer at Salomon had I not been ousted, so I was delighted to find that the move to Credit Suisse brought with it a host of benefits. As a greenfield analyst—the term used to describe firm-grown talent—I had never experienced the kind of instant respect I felt when I started at Credit Suisse. I was plied with perks that made me feel I was really rising through the ranks, that I was truly making it.

I was perhaps most dazzled by having access to a driver who would cart me around the city to my various meetings or else drive me to the airport; and not just any driver, but Mostafa, or Moe as I came to know him. From the moment he stepped into my life over twenty years ago, he made me feel like a princess. He's there to open my door and usher me into buildings with an umbrella overhead when it's raining. When

I slide into the back seat after a long day of meetings, there's a bowl of fruit waiting for me. When it's cold, I'm handed tea. While in the beginning, I basked in feeling important and being pampered in such a way, I soon came to view Moe as not just my driver, but my good friend. He's well read and clever and became a valuable sounding board for my worries, both personal and professional. In fact, he became such a trusted companion that once, when I was in New York with Zoey, my oldest child, when she was five months old, I handed her off to Moe with instructions to feed and burp her while I ran into Barney's to buy a few things. That may sound odd to others but, with our bond, it didn't feel like a strange request to either of us; Moe was and is an integral part of my life, still carting me wherever I need to go to this day. He and his wife Ellen are family. Riding around with Moe or his drivers are some of the best parts of my visits to New York City. We chat and I try to learn about them, offering ways to build personal wealth for these hardworking men and women. A few minutes educating drivers about the stock market could forever change their lives. Now that is a high!

But I didn't know that would be the case back in '97 when we met. Then, it was about getting my first true taste of what Wall Street success feels like. The salesforce at Credit Suisse treated me like a rock star. I had been forced to test my market value and I was elated with what I found.

Joint and Several Liability

One of my first big calls at Credit Suisse came just a few years after I was hired. During the late 1990s, there were a lot of lawsuits about the use of asbestos. People had known for decades the damage that asbestos could do, but it wasn't until the 1980s and '90s that a flood of litigation hit over the building material's ability to cause fatal diseases such as mesothelioma and lung cancer. These suits would eventually reach over $200 billion in damages in the United States alone, but no one could have predicted the eventual scope in the early days. When I came onto the scene, analysts and investors were attempting to quantify the risk for the companies that produced and sold asbestos. Some of those companies fell into my coverage universe, including Armstrong World, Owens Corning, and US Gypsum (USG)—all three of which were at the center of the storm. I took a more cautious stance on the stocks at the time which was considered a contrarian call.

One of the challenges of determining the impact that the litigation would have on the companies was something called joint and several liability; the law basically states that even if you didn't make and sell the specific asbestos that someone got sick from, you were still liable if you had ever produced it so long as your business was still in existence. This made things much more onerous for the manufacturers that were still around as many of the asbestos manufacturing companies had folded over the years. Given the scale of what we were up against, I had my Cleveland associate, Jason Putman, a lanky Michigan State graduate, working closely alongside me. He was hardworking and independent, and we made a great team. In his first few months, we toiled tirelessly to learn as much as we could about asbestos and cold-called many lawyers to better understand the implications of joint and several liability.

Jason and I tackled big questions about the laws and their fair inter-pretation. If a company only manufactured $10 million of asbestos, did it make sense for them to be liable for billions of dollars in damages just because their organization was still around? Were they getting punished for having succeeded as a business? Further, being held liable wouldn't just kill a company, but put hundreds of employees out of work. On the other hand, twenty-seven million American workers had asbestos exposure from 1940 to 1980 alone; tens of thousands of them had died, with many more becoming sick and incapacitated. The diseases caused by asbestos are horribly painful to suffer and it only seemed fair that someone had to pay.

As I pressed on in my research, the head of legal for Owens Corning, Maura Abeln Smith, invited me out to dinner one night. She said she wanted to help me better understand the nature of the litigation, and perhaps encourage me to change my negative stance on her company and the other companies affected. She'd bring along an expert on the subject, she said.

We met at Nicola's on the Upper East Side, one of my favorite restaurants. It was a quaint Italian bistro with stone floors, stucco walls, and closely packed tables. I got there early, so I sat at the small bar. There was just one other guy there and we struck up a conversation. As it turned out, it was Mike Rozen, the special master in asbestos and Maura's expert guest.

He explained to me that a special master is someone appointed by a judge to hear evidence and make recommendations in cases like this one where there was an abundance of different class action lawsuits. The plaintiff attorneys were going around to different parts of the country, aggregating as many people as possible who were sick or had died from asbestos so that they could sue the defendants. Mike's task was to act as the intermediary, and to try to figure out ways the whole thing could be settled.

Once Maura arrived, she set Mike to the task of trying to convince me the companies were mitigating the risk imposed by these lawsuits. Mike's overview that night was certainly an education, but not one that left me with a more constructive view of Owens Corning. In fact, the more I heard, the less confident I became that the involved companies were ever going to make the plaintiffs content.

As the dinner wrapped up, Mike and I exchanged our contact info. Every time there'd be a new development in the litigation, we'd talk it through. He provided an impartial perspective on the endless number of lawsuits that had been filed and were still coming down the pipeline. While that dinner started a process that eventually ended up cementing my negative views, Mike and I went on to become good friends.

The Love of Puzzles

With Mike's assistance, Jason and I were able to dig in further, contacting plaintiff firms in order to speak to them directly. The firms revealed to us that the number of lawsuits was accelerating at a robust pace. We now had key knowledge simply because we asked for it; companies were required to disclose new cases filed against them every quarter, so it was public information. The numbers we were seeing conveyed the overwhelming magnitude of the liability that was going to come to fruition. In addition to the sheer quantity of cases, there was a quality of personal payback in the flavor of the proceedings. It didn't seem to be about money for many of the plaintiff clients. We heard USG say things like: "We are working on a settlement." But a plaintiff would counter with: "There's no way in hell we're settling anything with them. They can't pay us enough." Looking at the filings both in terms of the quantity and their tenor, it was clear the balance sheets of these companies would not be able to withstand the looming massive liabilities.

This was not a well-received conclusion. I remember being in the middle of giving a presentation at T. Rowe Price in Baltimore during this period, when I was abruptly interrupted by a secretary.

"Ivy, you have a phone call. It's urgent," she said.

I left the room at a brisk pace, anxious to know what was going on. I had hardly picked up the phone before I heard the low, threatening voice of the head of investment banking.

"Young lady, do you know where your bread is buttered?" he asked.

Owens Corning was an important client of the firm, and he was upset I hadn't recommended their stock. In fact, he made it clear he wanted me to upgrade the stock. It seemed that Owens Corning had been complaining to their investment bankers about the analyst who was causing them such a headache. And so it was that the head of investment banking took it upon himself to figure out exactly where I was and talk to me immediately, my presentation be damned. Despite his intensity,

I didn't back down; I didn't upgrade the stock. I refused to capitulate to the fact I was told I had to do something or else be in trouble. I'd be lying if I said I wasn't intimidated by the way I was being spoken to, and that I had been so brusquely called out of a meeting for the conversation to take place, but I knew caving was out of the question.

Why were we willing to rock the boat in this manner? Because we were sure of what we were seeing. There is no substitute for the kind of leg work that went into arriving at our conclusion on the asbestos-impacted stocks. It required hours and hours of effort, through nights and weekends. We had to make the right calls, read the precise reports, reach out to the key people, and persist even when we seemed to be hitting nothing but dead ends. This is where passion becomes crucial. When you are passionate about your work, you don't worry about the time it's taking. You worry about doing the job as best as you can. I always experienced an excitement around making big calls that fueled me. It's only the uninspired who start up with *the weekend can't get here soon enough rhetoric*. When there's intellectual discovery, when you're in it, you're alive, and there's no better high.

It's like when I'm doing a puzzle with my youngest daughter, Zia. We'll be talking and laughing as we hunch over the table putting pieces in their rightful place. Often, we're shocked to realize we've been sitting there staring at the table for ten straight hours while the rest of the family long ago went to bed. I'll notice I didn't take a single sip of my wine the entire time; we were in the zone, and we had fully lost ourselves there. That's exactly how it felt to tackle a big problem as an analyst. It was never a chore. The long hours were worth the thrill of watching something come together piece by piece and knowing that I was the one who had orchestrated it.

Warren Buffett Doubles Down

The deeper we dug, the clearer things became and the more convinced I was that I was right to be negative in my call on these stocks.

But then, Warren Buffett bought 15 percent of USG's outstanding shares. Based on that news, USG's stock appreciated 30 percent to $19.375 per share. It was August 2000 and I was home on maternity leave with my oldest daughter, Zoey, when I got a frantic call from Jason relaying that USG's stock was skyrocketing. I had purposefully been trying not to check stock prices every day. My daily mood was too dependent on how the stocks traded, even if the change had nothing to do with anything fundamental; it was too much of an emotional roller coaster. I was taking the opportunity presented by my maternity leave to try to cultivate some healthy distance, but we now had a crisis on our hands. Everyone assumed that Buffett must know something that we didn't for him to take such a decisive stake in the company. My sales force quickly lost confidence in my negative call and nervously checked in with me to see what I thought.

What I thought was that Buffett hadn't done the work. He had a conceptual position; he wanted to own high-quality companies in the building product space that had strong brands. He owned, or would later own, many companies that fit this profile: Benjamin Moore, Johns Manville, Berkshire Hathaway Home Services. He believed that USG was a dominant company with high market share. He also owned some of USG's corporate debt, so this was an effort to double down to protect himself.

Remember that frenzied call to Ruth? I needed to speak to Mike, and I needed to speak to him right away. I didn't have to ask twice. Ruth hustled to pull Mike out of the meeting he had been in. I was not at my most articulate. "Mike, what the fuck?"

He knew, of course, what I was talking about. "Stick to your guns, Ivy. You know more than anyone else out there. You know more than he does. You're going to be right."

He could feel my anxiety through the phone.

"I mean it," he said. "Go hang out with your daughter."

That single phone call settled me down like nothing else could've. I knew I could trust Mike. I knew he knew what he was talking about. We had done our hard work, our due diligence, and that was all that mattered.

Nobody else seemed to believe me. My colleagues were worried, convinced I was going to be wrong. But I took Mike's advice—I stuck to my guns and ignored the rising clamor of voices contradicting what I had researched. Even the one that belonged to Warren Buffett.

It was my job and my responsibility to tell our clients what was going on in the market. I firmly believed the companies wouldn't survive what was coming, and so that is what I had to report. Buffett, on the other hand, saw a cheap stock and a strong brand, and so he acted. It turned out to be one of the biggest public mistakes he's made over the course of his entire career.

Asbestos litigation became the longest, most expensive tort in U.S. history. Armstrong World, Owens Corning, and US Gypsum were just three of the many publicly traded companies that were bankrupted in the fallout. Getting this major call right cemented my leadership position in the housing space and taught me a pressure-packed lesson in believing in myself.

Chapter Six

FAMILY FIRST
(EVEN IF IT MEANS MOVING TO CLEVELAND)

"Are they talking to me?"

When I was a little girl, I always dreamed I would live in New York City. I wanted to follow in my father's business footsteps—and that meant living in the Big Apple. If you had asked me: "Do you see yourself living in New York forever?" I think I would have said "Yes." If you had asked me: "Do you see yourself moving to Cleveland?" I'm sure I would have laughed out loud. *Absolutely not!*

But then I fell in love with David.

Living in New York suited me. I thrived on the electric current that hummed through the crowded Manhattan streets. It seemed like the city was made up of the best and the brightest, and it motivated the hell out of me. I wanted to belong among the incredibly ambitious people surrounding me. It truly felt like if you could make it in New York, you could make it anywhere, and I loved that. When presented with the option of moving to Cleveland, David's hometown, I worried that I would lose my edge as I softened into a suburbanite three hundred miles away from all the action. I prayed that my boss Jack Kirnan would reject my request to move when the time came. To my horror, he gave his hearty support, congratulating me on my pregnancy and promising that Credit Suisse would even set up a Cleveland office space for me.

So it was with immense relief that I found, even after moving to Ohio, that I was still Ivy, and I was still a force to be reckoned with in the industry.

Every reservation I had about the move melted away as soon as I got there. It was June of 2000 when I first called Cleveland home and I was seven months pregnant. Once I was a mother, I even more deeply appreciated living in a spacious house and having a car. Suddenly, going to the store felt easy and I had access to an amazing outdoor experience that I completely missed out on in New York City.

To make the transition even easier, I was still able to visit New York all the time so I felt I truly had the best of both worlds. If Credit Suisse wanted me there, I'd get on a plane and go. These trips were always fun and gave me the chance to revamp my wardrobe with better fashion choices than were available in my new city, but they also unexpectedly helped me embrace Cleveland life even more wholeheartedly. When I visited New York, I was reminded of the parts of life there I had hated like the traffic and the guarded nature of the people. By contrast, I remember getting on an elevator in Cleveland and a few fellow riders saying, "Good morning!" I literally looked around behind me like: "Are they talking to me?" That friendliness was foreign to me, and I loved it.

Life in Cleveland also reminded me of why I fell in love with David. Chief among his many wonderful qualities is his loyalty to his family and his friends.

From our first real conversation at Salomon, David's adoration for his close-knit family was clear. He called his mother daily to check in and often talked about his family's famous Sunday-night dinners where his siblings and all their kids gathered at his parents' house to consume massive amounts of good food and catch up on the week. It sounded overwhelming and chaotic to me at first, being so different from my family dynamic, but I couldn't help but think what a fantastic environment it would be to raise children in. When David first mentioned that his parents, his siblings, and their children all vacationed together, I was shocked. At the time, my family seemed entirely disengaged by comparison. I yearned for the kind of family experience he described and, as David and I grew closer and our relationship became more serious, the Zelmans' world opened up to me.

When I first met David's parents his father, Jerry, intimidated me. His strong presence and tough aura, underpinned by the stories David told me about him being a strict disciplinarian, made it clear he was not a man to be messed with—as did the gold necklace he wore in the shape of a U with a screw through it. But while he may have come off as threatening, I came to find he is a big softy who adores his daughter-in-law.

It's clear David absorbed his family-first mentality in large part from his father. Jerry was, and is, fiercely committed to looking after the members of his family. He's chivalrous and old-fashioned in charming ways—I learned quickly never to try to pick up the tab when Jerry was around—while also more than happy to celebrate and support each of the successes brought to the family table.

Harriet, David's mother, the matriarch of the family, ran her own headhunting firm called Satellite at the time I first started visiting Cleveland. Jerry wholeheartedly supported her career, even working alongside her doing the payroll for a time. While he was traditional in some ways, he didn't have an ego when it came to family. He also seemed to be proud of me and my success, a fact he made clear from my first visit. I had appeared on CNBC recently and Jerry was excited to show me a picture he had taken of my face floating on their family TV. From day one, Jerry and Harriet welcomed me with open arms, and I relaxed into the fact they were happy that David and I were together.

I was elated to finally participate in one of the Zelman family dinners but, even after the many stories I'd been told by David, I was blown away by what constituted a normal Sunday night for this family. It wasn't a holiday or any special occasion and yet Harriet put out a massive spread including steaks, hamburgers, hot dogs, chicken breasts, and a range of side dishes. To this day, I remember the pita chips; they were laced with garlic and butter, and they were the best thing I had ever tasted. But Harriet was more than a great cook; she was a sharp, astute businesswoman who fueled her four children's self-confidence and self-respect. She was a force to be reckoned with. When David's siblings, Dan, Darcy, and Debby arrived with their bustling families, I looked at David wide-eyed as everyone gathered around the kitchen counter piling their plates full of whatever they could get their hands on.

Connecting with David's three siblings and their families, all of whom lived in the immediate area, felt less intimidating and even natural with a plate of delicious food balanced on my lap. The vibe of the entire evening was warm and inclusive, and I felt at ease. The evening reminded me of the Cunninghams from the 1970s sitcom *Happy Days*, or of Mayberry, the fictional North Carolina town in *The Andy Griffith Show* from the '60s. I realized with a laugh these old shows were my only field of reference because I genuinely didn't realize families like this and communities like this actually existed. I couldn't believe I was now part of it.

Loyal to the End

As the weekend progressed and I went on to meet David's friends, the dreamlike quality of the visit persisted. David went to school, from the elementary years through to college, with the same group of guys. To this day, most of his buddies have been by his side since the earliest days; one of his best friends, Adam, was born the same week in the same hospital as David and they're still inseparable. Even with having certain long-standing friendships of my own, I was deeply moved by witnessing David's commitment to his lifetime circle of friends. Furthermore, my maternal grandma, Ruthie, whom I adored, schooled me to only date men who had good friends.

David arranged a dinner for me to meet his core group which included Adam, Warren, Roy, Darryl, Brucie, and Harley. I couldn't help but be nervous walking into a group of such established relationships as the new girlfriend. But as with the Zelmans, my worries were in vain. The men and their partners were warm and inviting and I was immediately accepted into the fold.

So really, it was from my first visit that I started to legitimately envision a life in Cleveland. If David and I decided to start a family together, the kind of support available to us in Ohio would be hard not to choose. The thought of having a built-in family and being able to step neatly into David's existing friend group was incredibly appealing. Yet despite how wonderful my first visit was, I still didn't really believe I was going to move there. But that trip to Cleveland turned into another, and then another. Meanwhile, David's friends and family started taking more frequent trips to see us in New York City. We even met up with David's brother, Dan; Dan's wife, Ellen; and their kids in Los Angeles to spend part of our vacations together. I felt like I was being incorporated into the family in a real way. My relationship with Jerry and Harriet grew especially strong; they treated me as if I was their own daughter and never failed to make me feel deeply loved.

When we finally committed and made the move to Cleveland, I was surprised by how well I fit right into Zelman family life. The healthy, robust dynamic was still novel to me and while I treasured it, it could be overwhelming at times. Certain Sundays, I just wouldn't feel like being surrounded by twenty clamoring voices. David would laugh at me and say, "No matter how you feel now, you'll talk more than I do when we get there." And he was right; I always happily melted into the chaos. No matter what was going on in our lives, we became active participants in that Sunday night tradition.

The concept of traditions, especially weekly ones, was new to me and I enjoyed learning how to embrace consistency and make room for new things. This extended to practicing religion. Although I was Jewish, I hadn't been raised with any religious teachings and didn't know much about Judaism before I married David. The extent of my Jewish experience to that point had been Passover dinners at my aunt's house in childhood, where I was more concerned with building forts with my cousin, Janet, who I'm still very tight with to this day—than I was absorbing the meaning of the occasion. But as David and I grew our family together, that changed. In addition to taking our children to Sunday School and attending high holy days services, David started the tradition of having Shabbat dinner at our house every Friday night. It has been a mainstay throughout the years and something our three children have grown to love; while there was occasionally reluctance in their teenage years when they'd rather spend Friday night with their friends, there is no whining or complaining now. Instead, we sit together around the table, with usually one of their friends as a guest or my sister Ally and her family, feasting and talking about our weeks with loud voices and lots of laughter.

It's been remarkable to watch the way in which David's loyalty to his community has expressed itself over the course of decades. He isn't only present for celebrations, the births and the marriages, but he is also steadfast about showing support in the hard times. Not out of a sense of obligation, but because he genuinely wants to—and this blanket of support extends wider for David than anyone else I've met. When the mother of one of his friend's wives died, there was no question that David would attend the funeral. He is never someone to simply send a note and some flowers. He is going to pay his respects in person. By the time of the funeral in question, I had been friends with his friends for twenty years and so I wanted to go too. It was as if I had picked up David's unshakable priorities by osmosis. He's someone who does the right thing, and now I try to as well.

Family First

I'm not trying to make David sound like a saint. Anyone who knows me knows that's not the case. There are just so many aspects of what it means to be truly present with family and what goes into building a happy and healthy home life that David was the first to teach me; these were things I had never learned growing up. David brought structure and intentionality into our home. He established traditions that came to define our family, making sure our children were respectful and considerate, and checking my priorities when they skewed too much toward work. There is no question he's been the foundation of our family.

From my first year at Salomon, I had grown accustomed to the grueling hours dictated by working on Wall Street. When I went back to work after having my first child, Zoey, it didn't explicitly occur to me I'd have to cut back. David was the one who would call me every day at 5:00 p.m. to ask, "Where are you? When are you coming home?"

"As soon as I can," I'd say.

He didn't like that answer, and I became used to his consistent pressure on me to prioritize quality time with our daughter. While my grueling travel schedule kept me away for a night or two per week and there were days I simply couldn't get away from work in time to make it home for dinner, I worked hard to be present when I was with Zoey. While David's constant criticism frustrated me at the time, I am so deeply grateful for his insistence that I shift my priorities.

Finding a healthy balance between career and family is a highly individualized endeavor and one that every parent with a demanding job needs to feel out for themselves. Over time, through trial and error—and occasionally even getting it right—I came up with guiding principles for myself. Once I had kids, I tried to only sleep away for as few nights as possible; when travel was a necessity, I made sure it never coincided with a child's birthday or major school event like a play, sporting event, or a recital. But still, even as I refined my process and began to find my stride, I struggled with the separation at times.

I found myself pulling out of the driveway with tears spilling down my face on more than one occasion, with guilt that I was once again leaving overwhelming me. While the dark skies cloaked the early morning hour, I'd kiss my sleeping children's foreheads goodbye, sniffling the entire drive to the airport. In these moments, I was again struck by a deep gratitude for Moe. He would soothe me as we drove, helping me cope with the trauma of leaving my children behind. He had been part of my life from before I was even married, and he was around to watch each of the kids grow up in turn. I was grateful for his steadfast presence as I navigated the challenges of being a working mother.

Once I got to the airport, I'd have to wash my smeared makeup off in the bathroom. I was grateful to know my children were in good hands; my sister Ally was their caretaker for eleven years and it did my heart good to leave them with family. Nonetheless, those were some of the hardest mornings I can remember. But then, on the flip side, coming home was incredible. The kids would be waiting on the driveway to welcome me home with hugs and kisses, big smiles, and shining eyes. The homecomings grew even sweeter as the kids aged—until, of course, they were old enough they had full lives of their own and hardly noticed I was back. Then, it was only my beloved Australian shepherds, ZZ and Zilli, jumping with joy to welcome me home. Bittersweet, perhaps, but as it should be.

Now, I intensely value being able to call Cleveland home. Over the last twenty-plus years, I've raised my family with strong values, rooted in a community that makes all of us proud to be Clevelanders. While it may not be Mayberry, it's not far off from Mayberry either. It's been an amazing environment to raise my family and I'm grateful David got us out of New York City. Even if I don't live here full-time for the rest of my life, I will always have a base in Cleveland. It's important to me that when my children come home after a semester of college or for holidays well into the future, they have their bedroom waiting for them. Finding myself out on my own at eighteen, I didn't have that, and I envied those who did. Seeing how the support and stability of their family contributed to the success of David and his siblings was evidence enough for me that kids, and then young adults, benefit from having a home to go back to as a necessary transition to being totally on their own—just one of the many lessons learned from the Zelmans and Cleveland.

Chapter Seven

STICK TO YOUR GUNS
(NO MATTER WHAT NAMES THEY CALL YOU)

"When you look in the mirror, it shouldn't be Ivy Zelman, the housing analyst. It should just be Ivy Zelman."

Once I found my way at Credit Suisse, I rose to become the #1-ranked housing analyst and went on to hold the prestigious position for almost a decade. It wasn't until I turned bearish on my coverage universe that I fell back to number three—supplanted by a classic bull on housing. I wasn't against anyone being a bull—just as I didn't intentionally set out to be bearish at the time—but my analysis and channel checks supported my cautious stance.

Losing my #1 ranking from *Institutional Investor* left me deeply rattled. I had grown so accustomed to being formally recognized as the best in the industry that I was unsure of how to proceed without the affirmation. When I confided in my father how hard I was struggling over the reshuffle, he said words I have never forgotten: "When you look in the mirror, it shouldn't be Ivy Zelman, the housing analyst. It should just be Ivy Zelman."

It sounded like good advice. I could recognize that, but I had no idea how to begin to apply it. If I was going to "just be Ivy Zelman," I needed to figure out who that was. If she wasn't the #1-ranked analyst, then who was she? I wrestled with my answers to this question for some time. While losing the top spot was tough, it triggered deep reflection that helped me find self-identity outside of the ranking system. While before, I had craved outside recognition and used it to establish my self-image, I was beginning to accept that being the top-ranked analyst had no material impact on my life or my worth. The world didn't end. It didn't affect my employment status or how my friends felt about me. Because I enjoy what I do and crave excellence, I continued to work hard and give my job my all; but my motivation had shifted, and it had a spillover effect on other areas in my life.

The shift in my perspective was buoyed by my realization of how biased the rankings were. Losing the #1 position had nothing to do with my performance. Instead, it was a reflection of my no longer working at a huge institution with a massive sales force to solicit votes, as well as the fact that many investors who owned the stocks I was bearish on wouldn't support me. They were doing exceptionally well at the time and didn't like the message I was delivering. By the time I eventually reclaimed the #1 spot after being vindicated with my big call, it felt inconsequential. The high it used to give me had been replaced by a steady, internally originated confidence—and I was just fine with that.

In truth, there was little time to worry about rankings when faced with the reality that the housing bubble was going to burst. To me, it was clear it wasn't a question of if but when. As early as November 2004, my associates and I were concerned affordability had grown too stretched as home appreciation soared. However, very few investors—or even my internal sales force—wanted to hear my concerns. It was as if we were the sober ones at a raging party; we may have been trying to shut it down before disaster hit, for the good of all, but that didn't change the fact we were trying to kill the good times happening now. The risks mounted as the party raged on. My anxiety deepened even as housing stocks rallied and outperformed all other sectors for over a year. Public builders stuck to the party line that housing was in a "secular shift," wanting to believe that current demographics would continue to drive homeownership to 70 percent of the population, well above the norm. But at the same time, most private builders worried the market wasn't sustainable, especially given how many investors were buying new homes.

While I received plenty of direct skepticism, I also knew that management teams were making fun of me behind my back. I learned that some had taken to calling me Jihad. I wasn't sure what it meant, but I was told it was because I was "at war against the housing industry," making it an offensive nickname on many levels. I also heard Poison Ivy on a regular basis. Other investors stuck more to market lingo and called me a "permabear" but, while less offensive, it wasn't an accurate term either. A permabear is always waving red flags, permanently negative about the future direction of the markets and the economy in general, no matter what. That was never the case with me or my team. Rather, our fundamental work and thorough research were reflected in our calls.

A good analyst shouldn't skew bullish or bearish. It's not our job to be either a worrywart or a cheerleader. Instead, we perform value-add analysis and provide guidance to our clients and industry executives based on thoughtful and thorough research. By late 2004 into mid-2005, it was exceedingly clear to me the market was headed down a dangerous road at an unsustainable speed. The only logical outcome was a crash. I knew I had to stick to my guns, even if it hurt my career in the short-term.

Role of the Anecdotal

As an analyst I was well acquainted with the metrics that indicated the health of the housing market; when they all started signaling distress, I couldn't help but be cautious. The lack of affordable housing was the most glaring problem, with affordability indexes the lowest on record. To combat this, the chairman of the Federal Reserve Board, Alan Greenspan, in February 2004, advocated the use of adjustable-rate mortgages (ARMs) to offset the high cost of standard home loans. This was the first catalyst that contributed to the strong momentum evidenced in 2004. As their name would indicate, adjustable-rate mortgages provided a lower monthly payment initially but adjusted upward after a short period, presenting the risk that monthly payments could increase to unsustainable levels. Despite this risk, Greenspan's willingness to give ARMs his blessing was interpreted as a go-ahead for lenders to introduce all kinds of exotic products into the mortgage market. The goal was to create an artificially affordable environment, and it worked; the market was driven to exuberant levels. Soon, consumers were getting approved for loans based on little more than a vague idea of what they were going to be able to afford in the future rather than on what they could presently afford. With no proof of income needed, these became known as "liar loans."

In the thick of this problematic swell in lending, I met a mortgage originator in my network for lunch. He told me he had just approved a loan to a young law graduate who had passed his bar exam but didn't yet have a job lined up.

"Why in the world would you lend him money if he doesn't have a job yet?" I couldn't help but ask.

He laughed. "Well, he will someday, and besides Fannie or Freddie will buy it from me—so what do I care?"

He was talking about the guidelines under which Fannie Mae and Freddie Mac, the government-sponsored entities (GSE), permitted lenders to underwrite loans because they knew that they had U.S. taxpayers as a backstop. One such program was called Fast and Easy—a name which should send up red flags in and of itself, really. Fast and Easy was developed by Countrywide and required borrowers to provide little or no documentation about their finances. They didn't have to produce pay stubs or tax forms to document earnings. In many cases, Countrywide didn't even require employment to be verified. It started an alarming trend, with every lender following suit and launching similar programs of their own, knowing the GSEs would buy the loans with the government's stamp of approval.

While an analyst focuses most heavily on data, there are other important techniques that help to keep one's finger on the pulse of what's going on in any given sector. This is where anecdotal evidence comes into play. Because of my inquisitive nature, I have always been naturally suited to collect such soft evidence and add it to the hard data of spreadsheets and algorithms. When I am out and about, whether officially on business or not, I look to blend the data I've collected with what I'm seeing with my own eyes. I might ask a taxi driver: "How's the local economy?" Or if I'm getting my nails done, I'll ask the women at the salon: "What's the unemployment rate like around here?" If you weight them properly, these insights can be a valuable addition to the figures coming from operators in the field and can push you down a new path to investigate.

What I witnessed at lunch with that mortgage originator was just one of the many stories I was hearing about housing in those days that were too good to be true; they were coming from everywhere. It felt like every person I encountered had a story about making fast money from buying and flipping homes with no money down at ridiculous teaser rates, or through loans with option ARMs that would reset to higher rates down the road. In the cities I traveled to across the country, waitresses, hairdressers, and bellboys alike were happy to regale me with tales of how many houses they had bought.

The situation became alarmingly real to me in 2005. David and I were in Rosemary Beach, Florida, relaxing on the beach when a guy who was renting out umbrellas struck up a conversation with my husband. It turned out he wanted David to buy some lots with him nearby. In the previous week, a lady at the nail salon and my trainer at the gym had both told me they, too, were buying lots. The momentum had reached a fever pitch. This was not data generated by a computer; these were real life examples, and they were everywhere. With all the hallmarks of a classic bubble, there was no denying this was real.

The trip left me shaken and reinforced my need to stay bearish. The surveying of my private contacts, careful consideration of the data, and anecdotal evidence all worked to sharpen my perspective and give me more conviction about my position. Many of the private builders I relied on for their insights corroborated my opinion about the insanity of the market. Tom Krobot, then president and CEO of Ashton Woods Homes, a sizable private builder based in Atlanta, described an incident that exemplified my concerns. He was competing against public builders for a parcel of land.

Tom lost out on the land and was stunned when he found out what the winning bidder had paid. He called him up and asked, "How can you pencil a return on those lots at the price you paid?"

"I can't," the man answered. "But if I don't buy the land and provide volume, I'll get fired."

Wall Street investors wanted public companies to report strong top-line growth, and so those companies tied the compensation of their divisions' leadership to volume. In turn, the volume would create the kind of quarterly numbers that would propel their stocks higher, and everybody would be happy—putting staggering economic risk and soaring land inflation aside.

Investors Gone Wild

In July of 2005, my team and I pulled together everything we had observed and published a 50-page report called *Investors Gone Wild*. It was spiced up with some of our anecdotal research, such as quotes from a mortgage broker ("If you can fog a mirror, you can get a home loan") and a home mortgage consultant ("A few years ago, you would have had to go to an infomercial to get the kind of deals we're offering now.") However, the bulk of our report featured hard data that detailed and quantified the percentage of investors who were purchasing homes, the markets that would be at significant risk when demand decreased to historical levels, as well as the risk to the market given housing's importance to the overall state of the economy. We also made sure to shine a light on all the exotic mortgage products the market was using to fuel housing's growth.

The report gave the issue of investors a special focus. While many homebuilders, real estate consultants, and analysts admitted that investors introduced an unhealthy dynamic to the marketplace, no one had yet been able to quantify the impact. To rectify this, we quantified the investor effect from a historical perspective while also being the first to gauge how investor euphoria could impact public homebuilders' margins, returns, and land assets. Using today's lingo, *Investors Gone Wild* went viral. People who were not only not on the distribution list, but also who weren't even directly involved in the industry, heard about it. When parents of my children's friends tell them "I've read your mom's research," there's a good chance this report is the one they mean.

We set up a conference call to discuss the findings of *Investors Gone Wild*. Normally, between 50 and 150 investors join us on these calls. This time around, the conference call company interjected just before we were set to begin: "You have 700 people on the line, and more dialing in. Do you want to wait, or start?"

By the time we started ten minutes later, over one thousand people had joined us to go through the material with accompanying slides. The presentation was thorough and largely met with stunned silence as no one had aggregated this type of framework before. It was a lot to digest. By the time the question-and-answer portion of the call came around, I was exhilarated. It was clear we had produced something that differentiated us from our competitors, while also quantifying and communicating extremely important insight to investors. We had created something proprietary, and the market was hungry for it. Our unbiased, independent perspective was and is the foundation for our credibility on Wall Street.

The interest in our work was broad. We weren't just speaking to equity investors in the housing space; rather, the people who dialed into our call spanned the entire market from fixed-income investors to asset-backed securitization professionals to private equity. Housing was the most important driver of the booming economy and the response to *Investors Gone Wild* proved that my team and I were on to something big. The victory was sweetened by knowing we had gotten there by compiling the right data and trusting our guts, no matter what names we were called or how we were publicly perceived.

To some degree, *Investors Gone Wild* was the culmination of the mammoth effort we had put into becoming the best team we could be. Without the support of the #1-ranking from *Institutional Investor*, without widespread affirmation or respect within the industry, we had accurately read the signs and trusted ourselves enough to stay the course even as we were ridiculed. The vindication of being proven right felt good but, while I was undoubtedly gratified, I had matured professionally, and I realized I didn't need external validation in the same way I had used to. Rather than letting praise define me again, I instead focused on the size of the interest in what we had to say. I started wondering, *how can I take this following and strike out on my own?*

Chapter Eight

TAKE THE HIGH ROAD
(BUT DON'T DRINK THE KOOL-AID)

"I'm sorry you don't like what I had to say.
But be careful. You better back up."

genuinely believe that those who can listen to their own counsel, and the counsel of those close to them—even as others actively root for them to be wrong—are prepared for almost any situation life throws at them. But while the ultimate victory was sweet, I don't want to minimize the long and lonely road that got me there. I came across doubters everywhere I went in those days. I'd overhear nasty whispers and mean-spirited jokes.

"Oh, sure, Ivy will be right . . . eventually. Like, years from now," they'd laugh.

Some were bolder and lobbed their doubts right in my face. I remember having lunch with a client in Boston and a salesperson from Credit Suisse.

When I voiced my severe housing concerns, the client said to me: "I hope you're right. I hope the stocks get killed so I can buy more."

I was stunned. "I don't meet too many clients who hope their stock has a 50-percent pullback so they can add to their position."

I glanced over at the salesperson, expecting him to chime in but he remained silent, siding with his client. As if what the client had said made any sense. Once again, I felt like I was the only sober person at the party.

As experiences like this stacked up, it became clear to me that money and greed have a way of clouding people's thinking. One evening, I had dinner in Cleveland at our local high-end restaurant, Red, with Richard Dugas, then-CEO of the PulteGroup, a leading public home builder. Looking across the table at me and accompanied by his CFO and head of investor relations, Richard told me: "Ivy, land prices don't go down."

I looked at him in disbelief. He reeked of confidence. In that moment, I remember realizing, *He really believes that.* It seemed people were bending economic laws to meet their own needs and assuage their own worries. I would debate the basics of our industry with the management teams on various earnings conference calls which were recorded and open to the public. On one such call, I got into a heated exchange with KBH's CFO during the question-and-answer session. I asked him how they would handle the risk of land prices going down and he responded by saying their land was a variable cost and that they would mitigate pressure by laying off additional purchasing.

I was floored. Land, like buildings, or machinery is a textbook example of a fixed asset. You can't just reconfigure economic theory to suit your own taste. If you were to dig up that recording, you'd hear me asking, "Why though? Why?" The response? "Ivy, just relax."

By this point in my career, I didn't have any problem telling people I thought they were out of their minds, even in a public forum. It wasn't personal; if their information wasn't accurate, I felt justified in telling them they were just flat-out wrong. It might not have won me many friends, but perpetuating the truth was more important.

Perhaps no situation more powerfully exemplifies this dynamic than the time I spoke at an event hosted by *Builder Magazine* in Santa Barbara. Everybody who was anybody in the industry was in attendance. I used the slides from the *Investors Gone Wild* report to talk about liar loans, the massive percent of lending being doled out to investors who were buying homes with no equity and no income verification. I named a publicly traded company, WCI, who was developing condos predominately in Florida and selling them to such investors. I made it clear I thought actions like WCI's were going to contribute to a major collapse in home prices.

I didn't know it, but the CEO of WCI at the time, Jerry Starkey, was in the audience. After I finished my presentation and climbed off the stage, Jerry charged toward me like a linebacker. He stopped short mere inches from me, and I realized I had been bracing my body for impact. He was so visibly and aggressively upset; I had genuinely thought he was going to knock me over.

I steeled myself. "You know what, Jerry? I'm sorry you don't like what I had to say. But be careful. You better back up."

While I had been shaken by having to consider, even for a second, that I could be physically assaulted, I couldn't help but laugh about it later over cocktails with Bruce Assam, the CEO of a private home-builder, and more important a good friend who I rely on to this day for his perspective on the market and also for good TV show recommendations. By then, the entire situation had become ludicrous to the point of being hilarious. It felt like the whole industry hated me. Jerry had been so angry, with true rage twisting his features. "Bruce," I said, "Should I be worried someone is actually going to take me out?" I was mostly joking. I hadn't yet received the anonymous fax with the threat that my fingers would be cut off if I didn't back down, you see. That delightful moment was yet to come. Still, all you can do sometimes is have another drink with a friend and laugh.

What About the Women?

Don't get me wrong; it's not that I go around looking for fights to pick, but if someone is trying to twist the facts or put me down unfairly, I'm going to defend myself. I didn't get where I was at this point by backing down from challenge or controversy. Naturally, over the previous decade and a half, that meant I had come across many men who attempted to discredit me or otherwise belittle my professional efforts. But women, too, unfortunately, weren't always kind; they were even mean-spirited at times. While you might think women would be more supportive of each other in a male-dominated industry—and maybe that is more so the case now—it was certainly not true in the mid-2000s. Having women high up in the finance world was still too new to have figured out how to get along, it seems. I grew accustomed to hearing that other women were talking about me behind my back, whether to clients or even the executives. I even had other women go so far as to call me their nemesis, which surprised me and felt unfounded. This animosity was the backdrop for what I have since dubbed The Great Debate, an event which took place in July 2005.

A portfolio manager for a major equity hedge fund asked me to come to their midtown office to participate in a debate. My opponent was a highly ranked housing analyst who had knocked me out of my #1 spot by remaining a classic bull all those years ago. While I had since made my peace with losing my ranking, I was excited to have this opportunity to vindicate my position to the person who had previously caused me so much angst.

Housing had become such an important force in the financial world, and the tension between players was so thick, that you could have filled an arena with spectators who were eager to see the showdown. It was a big deal, and I was grateful David had also been invited to fly to New York with me to view the debate as a guest. Malinda, my administrator, best friend, and deep woman of the world, came as well. There was mounting pressure and excitement in the days leading up to the event as I realized it would likely be a milestone in my career. I was glad David and Malinda would be there to share it with me.

David and I went out to dinner at Mr. Chow, a Chinese restaurant in New York City, the night before. While I had imagined the dinner as something to help me unwind before the big day, David was very intent at utilizing our quiet table; he coached me about the importance of retaining my poise on the following afternoon. I think he saw, perhaps more clearly than me, the potential for things to get ugly. While I expected everyone would retain the basic standards of professionalism, he wanted me to be prepared in case that didn't happen. Even if I was unfairly attacked, he urged me to stay calm and rise above it.

"Do yourself a favor," David said. "When you walk in there, the first thing you do is go over and shake her hand."

"No way!" I responded. "I'm not doing that."

David ignored me. "Don't interrupt her. Let her speak. Don't get upset, no matter what she says."

While I was mildly irritated by the conversation, it was valuable. I needed time to dwell on how to ask tough questions and be persistent while also heeding David's words of wisdom and making sure to show my opponent an appropriate level of respect.

"You need to be professional," he drilled into me. "Show her up with your skillset and you'll defeat any verbal abuse you might receive."

We'd find out shortly how prescient David's input was. The next day, I strode into the room and shook the hand of the woman I would be debating. We took our seats near large windows overlooking Fifth Avenue and Central Park. The view itself bespoke wealth and success and reflected the highly accomplished people in our industry who would be in attendance. The room was filled with the company hosting the debate's founder and his senior leaders, along with analysts and portfolio managers from across the country—while still more conferenced in. Housing was the most important driver of the economy and people realized they needed to better understand the overall trends in order to position their holdings in their funds.

In my briefing, I had been told my presentation should be high level rather than focusing on individual stocks. As such, I had pulled together slides from *Investors Gone Wild*. I spent time thoroughly preparing—out of respect for this client who had paid me—but also because I am committed to always doing the best job possible. There are things in your control, and things out of your control, and how well prepared you are for something important falls entirely in the former category.

My opponent had the floor first. I was surprised to find she had no slides prepared and she spoke only about individual stocks. I wondered if she got the same memo from our host that I did. As she jumped from topic to topic, seemingly without a grand plan, it seemed that if she had, she decided it would be easier to skim the surface of the situation our industry was in rather than offer a comprehensive take.

I smiled to myself, feeling my confidence increase as to who was going to win this debate. When it was my turn, I handed out my slides and began walking the group through our material.

Not long after I started, I heard an audible snort. I paused briefly, but then continued. Just ten slides into my presentation, I heard an outburst from the woman I was debating.

"All the companies think her research is crap!"

I froze, unsure if the interruption had happened. Surely, she wasn't so shameless, I thought. With David's words in mind, I took a deep breath and said, "Well, okay . . ." and carried on with my presentation, ignoring her gratuitous interruption. When I finished, our host asked us for our best idea, long or short. My opponent recommended a buy on Centex, the largest builder at the time. I suggested shorting KBH given that they were the most exposed to the markets with the greatest investors out West. I hardly finished my sentence before I heard her loud voice once again.

"The stock is up 700 percent since you downgraded it," she said. She dropped her voice just slightly, making sure it would still carry across the room, "And it will keep going up in your face!"

I scanned the crowd until I found David's face; even he looked shaken. Somehow, I managed to keep my cool through the end of the meeting, until the three of us burst out of the building back into the summer heat. We went to BLT Steak for lunch on 57th Street. While it's one of my favorite restaurants and was meant to be a celebration, I took no pleasure from the experience. I knew we had something of a professional rivalry, but I was startled at how nasty my opponent had been and, as I had more time to process, I was angry. David tried to console me, telling me that my restraint had made me look professional and her foolish by comparison.

He was right. The feedback from our client was that I had clearly won the debate. It was mere months later that I reclaimed my #1 ranking as the cracks in the housing market grew more apparent. Suddenly, the momentum shifted. I gained recognition by The Street for staying the course on my bearish call. Even though many still didn't agree with our controversial call, clients across Credit Suisse's vast departments wanted to meet with me. In retrospect, The Great Debate came just as I was cresting the longest and most intense professional wave I would experience over the course of my career.

A Roller Coaster of a Ride

While July of 2005 marked a key turning point in my career, the next few years proved to be a long-distance race rather than a sprint. A race that I very much enjoyed; it was more satisfying than anything I had before felt from a career perspective. Housing stocks began to tank in the latter half of 2005, even as the overall market remained strong.

Homebuilding stocks plunged over 40 percent before bottoming out in the fall of 2006. Rising resale activity and new-home inventory drove builders to turn to incentives to compel buyers back to the market. Home prices were under pressure and builder margins began to compress.

While many investors were still not grasping the enormity of what would soon unfold, there were a few who were aligned with our team's bearish call. Steve Eisman, the portfolio manager at Frontpoint and his team, including Brad Berning, his analyst, called me daily to exchange stories. Prior to the housing market slowdown, Steve had gone to the asset-backed securitization housing conference in Las Vegas which had over five thousand participants. He left with crazy stories about how everyone, down to the parking attendant at the hotel, was buying houses. Allen Puwalski, an analyst at Paulson, also called daily as they also had a massive short call on the sector.

In October 2006, we published another large, thematic report entitled *Wonder-Land*. One of the conclusions of the one-hundred-page study was that builders would be forced to write off 20 percent of their equity given that land prices were currently overvalued and would surely plunge. Directionally we were right, but we didn't go far enough; builders would wind up writing off *55 percent* of their equity after all the dust settled. While we were wrong on the amount, no one else was even contemplating land being written off.

As we wrote then, it all starts with land; land is a homebuilder's lifeblood. The difference between a great project and an average project is often determined by how astutely the land was purchased. This inherent risk, and potential for a big mistake, is why many CEOs of public builders have tighter reins on land investment than any other part of their organizations. We tried to understand every important component of the land business, including how it was intertwined with the homebuilders' operations and what implications it carried for asset and stock market valuations. What we found was that the market had yet to find a bottom and builders were burning through their oldest and most profitable land while continuing to acquire more land at inflated prices. Well, not all builders, as many of the private builders that read our research stopped buying land given our warnings. To this day, I'm thrilled to hear from private builders, like my longtime friend Dwight Sandlin with Signature Homes in Alabama, that if it wasn't for our research, they would have gone bankrupt. This was honestly by far the most rewarding aspect of being right.

While housing corrections typically lead to economic downturns, we sensed that this time would result in far fiercer financial repercussions. As I've already said, my vindication did not unfold in a straight line. Rather it was a roller coaster, with exhilarating rises and terrifying dips. While homebuilding stocks declined for the first three quarters of 2006, they started rallying again following comments from the CEO of a public builder.

In the fall of 2006, Toll Brothers held their earnings call. Their cofounder and CEO, Bob Toll, claimed the housing market was improving. He offered the fact that they were seeing a pick-up in activity in the DC area as evidence. When it came time for the Q&A, I anxiously asked him: "What Kool-Aid are you drinking?"

Yet his gimmick seemed to work. Following the call, the Toll Brothers stock surged upward, as did other homebuilding stocks. Everyone wanted to believe that the downturn was over, and the bottom was behind us. We held the annual Credit Suisse housing conference soon after and the fact that we refused to go along with the new rhetoric reignited the industry's mockery of me. Stocks were up nearly 40 percent by the year's end. Word got back to me that people were calling this new uptick "the Zelman bottom."

I took a lot of heat for remaining bearish when people thought we should be more bullish. It wasn't only external investors, but those inside Credit Suisse who were starting to turn on me. The head of product management, Tim Landers, told me I should upgrade the stocks in early November as they kept climbing higher. Tim and I had a history of working well together; it was he who had hosted the call featuring *Investors Gone Wild* that saw over a thousand people dial in. Now Tim was telling me it was time to upgrade the stocks or else risk ruining my career. I should feel happy that I was right about the period that had just passed, he said, before adding that, "I should take my victory lap, and then get with the program." His efforts culminated in a long email, detailing examples of other analysts who were Permabears and wound up wrecking their careers.

I couldn't believe that kind of attack would come from inside my own organization. I knew that sometimes a sales force will go against your recommendations if their clients are putting pressure on them. I also understood that the stocks were going up, so some people internally were going to capitulate to these other forces. But it was still hard to comprehend that the product manager of Credit Suisse wanted me to ignore my fundamental research.

It struck me as ridiculous, even harassing, to receive this kind of unfounded opposition and intimidation from my own colleagues. I reported the situation to my boss, Stefano Natella, who was global head of research. He was supportive and told Tim to stand down. There were other traders and analysts who had my back as well, including John Cannon, a sales trader on the desk and Larry Sibley, a senior salesperson who unwaveringly encouraged me to stick to my guns. Their support, combined with my natural inclination not to back down from a fight, helped me regroup my energies, and then take it one step further.

Ten Reasons to Sell Homebuilding Stocks

By December of 2006, Dennis McGill, my senior associate, and I had had enough. We published a report entitled *10 Reasons to Sell Homebuilding Stocks* in which we moved our rating for the entire group of homebuilding stocks from neutral to underperform. We acknowledged that investors were enjoying a renewed rally, but we didn't believe the rationale for it was solid and felt sure the real pain had yet to come to fruition. The market was betting that the worst was over and, come spring, that housing would be back to a normal sales pace—possibly even with resumed pricing power. By contrast, we viewed the markets as very vulnerable and put a spring rebound at a low 20–25 percent probability. In fact, we said, the market could remain challenged throughout 2007, possibly picking up in early 2008.

We would prove to be more right than we could have even imagined. In this report, we reiterated our stance. Others may have felt we were pouring gas on the flames, but we didn't care what anybody else said. We knew things were going to get much uglier and we thought people should get the hell out of these stocks.

Dennis was the best ally to have at my side. While he was my associate at the time, he's now my partner. He started fresh out of Michigan as my summer intern before transitioning into a full-time employee at Credit Suisse. It didn't take long for me to think he might just be the smartest person I have ever met—despite his tall frame and boyish looks, his stoic charm fed my fire. He had a master's in accounting and was incredibly loyal to boot. In the early days, I used to take money out of my back pocket to pay him on top of what Credit Suisse did because I saw what an asset he was and felt he deserved more. I cared about him and wanted him to be rewarded for his hard work—and wanted to make sure he stuck around. Our strong bond then blossomed into a dynamic partnership down the road.

Dennis and I became like peanut butter and jelly—perfectly complementing. Dennis paired his admirable work ethic with stunningly original insights. Because he worked behind the scenes, he didn't get nearly as much public recognition as I did, but he was the driver of so much of the unique analysis we did. One of the lines I say all the time, even on stage at conferences is: "Dennis did all the work, I just take all the credit."

All joking aside, my success has been a team effort. When I make appearances as an expert on TV or nab the #1 ranking, I seem to be the one getting all the accolades; it's important to me that I'm clear I couldn't have done it without Dennis, Alan Ratner, or Justin Speer, all of whom rose from the position of summer intern to make crucial contributions to our office in terms of their research acumen and their camaraderie.

Alan is like a little brother to me. As with Dennis, I've watched Alan finish college, get married, and grow a family. I've also watched Alan, a University of Michigan alum, get mercilessly smack-talked by my Ohio State Buckeyes–loving husband. He truly takes everything with a smile. And yet, Alan is never a pushover. He has mastered the rare and invaluable art of being a deeply loyal team member while never veering into the territory of being yes-man. He's a sweetheart, but he's willing to challenge you. He's been with Zelman for sixteen years now, and he has never failed to work his ass off. I expect he'll be by my side for the rest of my career, and I feel fortunate that is the case.

Justin, for his part, was master of morale and played a key role in buoying the crew amid the trying times of the mid-2000s. He even made us all T-shirts that read "Mr. Housing Bubble"—a play on the Mr. Bubbles bath soap logo—which we took to wearing around the office. It was a reminder that we were on the same team, and that we were up against just about everybody else.

Underestimated No More

By the spring of 2007, our gradual vindication came to full fruition. Amid a surge in homeowner defaults, New Century filed for bankruptcy in March, a true sign of the slumping U.S. housing market. New Century was the largest independent U.S. provider of *subprime* mortgages, the term for home loans given to people with poor credit histories. More than thirty other companies in the same niche had sold or closed their doors in the year prior, but New Century was the biggest domino to fall; in 2006, they had been second only to HSBC Finance in issuing subprime mortgages. Now hardly a year later, New Century filing for Chapter 11 indicated the market was truly tanking. The housing bust has arrived.

History informed us that homebuilding stocks nearly always lead fundamentals, roughly six months ahead of time. It would not only be our sector that suffered. Lehman Brothers went on to collapse along with Bear Stearns. Fannie Mae and Freddie Mac, the two quasi-government public entities which bought and securitized mortgages for over 50 percent of the market, were taken into conservatorship by the U.S. government to keep the housing market functioning. Home prices were collapsing, falling over 30 percent from their peak in 2007 with millions of people losing their homes to foreclosure and short sales. The great recession was in full force and housing was at its center; the bottom was nowhere in sight.

If you saw the movie *The Big Short*, you might remember the scene where the two young investors who have bet heavily on the failure of subprime mortgage bonds have to endure an excruciating wait while the spike in defaults seems to leave the housing market unaffected. It was on April 2, 2007, that they learn of New Century's bankruptcy while watching CNN and realize the collapse of the market had begun in earnest. It was the moment for all of us.

Just three weeks before New Century's demise, we had published another thematic report called *Mortgage Liquidity du Jour: Underestimated No More*. The publication provided more detail on the dynamics of the mortgage market including the available products, the characteristics of the borrowers, and who the originators that wrote the loans were.

In response to the recent turmoil, we had surveyed our private home-builders and their mortgage lenders to assess the new home market's exposure to the mortgage products that were at greatest risk for increased regulation in the coming months; the findings showed it was not just a subprime issue. We believed that 40 percent of the market was at risk of significant fallout from tightening credit and increased regulatory scrutiny. We reminded investors that the headwinds from deteriorating credit would impact supply and pricing conditions, as well as incremental demand. With delinquency and foreclosure rates continuing to rise, more supply would be hitting the market. The impact of these issues would be felt throughout the entire market, regardless of builder price point, and would likely contribute to housing prices falling 30 percent or more.

Mortgage Liquidity du Jour cemented our dominant knowledge in the space. While we took some pride in knowing we had read and heeded the signs correctly, we were saddened real lives were at stake. The euphoria that convinced people home prices would go up forever created victims: old people persuaded to refinance by a shady mortgage originator, uneducated homeowners led to take cash out of their property in exchange for equity by their bank, aspiring young adults who bought property with no money down and ended up destroying their credit after being unable to make their payments.

As with any game of musical chairs, the music eventually stopped and there were not enough chairs for everyone scrambling to safety. I found some solace in being able to help the builders and other industry executives who listened to our advice. There are still companies that reach out to me today saying that, years ago, I saved them. They listened to my warning, and they stopped buying land. They believed me that the market was not sustainable. Knowing there are companies across the country that we helped mitigate the disaster for is what I'm most proud of. It's something that has contributed to my conviction that I need to stay true to my fundamental work and never back down from something I believe.

33. Ivy and Jennifer at Zia's birthday party (2016)

34. Zia, Zoey and Zach (2013)

35. ZZ and Zilli (2013)

36. Zelman family for Zia's Bat Mitzvah (2017)

37. Mom, Caryn, Dad, Ivy, Ally and Jerry Z. (2015)

38. Ivy, Zia and Mom at Zia's Birthday party (2011)

39. Ivy and Zia at Mr. Chow in Tribeca (2018)

40. Ivy and Ian (2006)

41. Ally, Ivy, Kim, Malinda and Dennis at Zoey's Bat Mitzvah (2013)

42. Ivy, Malinda and Dennis (2013)

43. Alan, Dennis, Jen (Alan's wife), Ivy, Malinda and boyfriend, Chris at Alan's wedding (2008)

44. Ivy and Yvette in Virginia (2016)

45. Ivy and Kim (2018)

46. Ivy and Dad (2019)

47. Ally and Ivy in Aspen (2019)

48. Leisa, Ally and Elena's kids and mine in London (2015)

49. Ivy and Leisa in London (2015)

50. Kim and Ivy in NYC (2018)

51. Jody and Ivy at Buckeye game (2016)

52. Ivy and Laura in Aspen (2018)

53. Ivy and Elena in Cyprus (2018)

54. Jennifer and Ivy at Cavs game (2018)

55. Dave, kids and I in South Africa (2017)

56. Ally, Ivy, Malinda and Kim in Cleveland (2019)

57. Ivy at Bergdorf's Goodman department store in NYC (2019)

58. Zoey at home in Cleveland (2019)

125

59. Zach at home in Cleveland (2019)

60. Zia playing soccer at WRA (2019)

61. Zia (2020)

62. Zia and Zach in Newport Beach (2021)

63. Zander and Zoso (2021)

64. Zilli reading The Wall Street Journal (2015)

Chapter Nine

GO OUT ON YOUR OWN
(BUT DON'T GO IT ALONE)

*"Hell," I thought, "if it doesn't work out,
I can always find a job."*

On October 3, 2007, the first anniversary of the publication of *Wonder-Land*, Dennis, David, and I launched our independent research boutique, Zelman & Associates, with Alan, Malinda, and Kim by our sides. We had several reasons for leaving Credit Suisse, but the primary catalyst was the unique opportunity we had on our hands with our proprietary research; we knew we could monetize the network we had built around it by hanging our own shingle at a higher level than Credit Suisse was willing to match. Before we left, we were swamped with requests from not only our own equity clients, but also clients from every other part of Credit Suisse: asset-backed securities, capital markets, fixed income, high yield. Yet the fact that our research was read and relied upon throughout the entire company was not reflected in our compensation. It seemed we were being undervalued. Combined with knowing we were in such high demand, it was clear the time was right to strike out on our own.

I was ready to move on for other reasons, as well. Given my independence, I wasn't well-suited to the bureaucracy of a big firm. My team and I often found ourselves venturing into someone else's territory as we dug into the underpinnings of the market, causing animosity with the professionals responsible for other silos. For example, the mortgage market was covered by another analyst, but it was necessary for us to analyze the space given how interrelated our sectors were. Specifically, the analyst who covered Fannie Mae and Freddie Mac felt strongly that I shouldn't be allowed to write about the GSEs—especially as I was negative, and he wasn't. This was a complaint also voiced on a nonsilo specific level; Credit Suisse's economic strategist constantly argued my negative view about home prices on internal conference calls, citing that home prices had never gone down in history and wouldn't start now. I boldly, but loudly, told her she was going to be wrong on multiple occasions. While I grew used to the workplace friction in some ways, it was exhausting having to stand my ground and constantly debate many among my in-house colleagues.

I understood that we were expected to stay in our lane, so to speak, but I was also committed to producing the most beneficial research possible and I felt strongly we couldn't effectively analyze homebuilding and building products in a vacuum. Understanding the state of housing was crucial to getting an accurate read on the rest of the market; investigating related industries gave my team a bird's-eye view of what was going on at every level. We knew our process of aggregating and triangulating information across sectors provided a differentiated perspective, one that the market needed. As a stand-alone firm, we would be able to branch out without stepping on anyone's toes to cover additional stocks that were part of the housing mosaic, including Home Depot and Lowe's, multifamily REITs, and mortgage-related stocks.

Comprehensive housing coverage, paired with our willingness to adopt a boots-on-the-ground approach, seemed like a surefire recipe for success. Very few had forecasted housing was going to bust, because just about everybody else relied on economic modeling. But economic models can't dig in the weeds, learning from owners and operators about the trends they're seeing play out in real life, not on computer screens. We put in the time-intensive fieldwork, talking with builders, mortgage companies, and real estate brokers. It was the secret sauce that topped off our unique value proposition.

The list of big-firm defectors who went on to successfully launch their own enterprises was not terribly long. Ed Hyman was perhaps the most well-known. He left C.J. Lawrence in 1991 to start his own firm and later sold it to Evercore for $400 million. Despite his success, few followed, and so I was grateful to be introduced to another trailblazer, Michael Goldstein, founder of Empirical Research. Larry Sibley, my favorite salesman who had full faith in my ability to pull this thing off, organized a dinner for the three of us in New York so I could hear about Michael's experience of starting his boutique firm a few years earlier.

The conversation was invaluable. I worked my way through what felt like an endless list of questions and left the dinner with pages full of notes. While Michael provided general insights, he also filled me in on some of the finer points of going out on my own. For example, he was insistent that we become a broker-dealer. We didn't want to set up an independent firm where we weren't regulated by the Financial Industry Regulatory Authority (FINRA). Having that regulation is what allowed Michael to be paid by the mutual funds who paid vendors with trading commissions, something he knew we'd need as well. Michael also impressed upon me the importance of building a trusted and skillful salesforce. To this end, I had been working on convincing Larry to join my endeavor for months, but he eventually opted not to leave the safe and stable environment of Credit Suisse. Even without having Larry to head my sales team, that dinner with Michael was the confidence boost I needed to pull the trigger. I left aware of how much work was ahead of me but felt surprisingly self-assured. *Hell*, I thought, *if it doesn't work out, I can always find a job.*

I knew the time had come, any way I looked at it. I had just turned forty and I was growing bored with where I was. I wanted more, and I certainly didn't want to grow stale. A man I greatly admired once told me that complacency is the next closest thing to death. I felt ready to challenge myself by no longer being part of a bureaucratic organization with built-in safety nets; perhaps more crucially, I had accepted the risk of failure, meaning I acknowledged its existence as a possibility even as I trusted it wouldn't be the outcome of the venture. My confidence had soared in recent years, and I had a team of trusted companions around me—including Dennis, Alan, and Malinda—who made me feel like I was the captain of a seaworthy ship. It might not be a huge craft, or a particularly fancy one at the start, but I had no doubt it'd be able to handle the rough waves of a market in turmoil.

Taking the Plunge

I applied my analyst methodology to my decision to leave Credit Suisse, basing the call on a blend of anecdotal evidence, research, and hard facts. While I was confident my network of industry contacts would support my entrepreneurial determination, caring more about my quality research than where I worked, I needed more substantive assurance. As such, I confidentially reached out to several clients to discuss my plans—theoretically, of course. I didn't explicitly say I was going to start my own research firm as that would have violated the terms of the noncompete and nonsolicit clauses in my contract. Instead, I asked people if I went out on my own "in theory," would they be willing to pay for my research? I was reassured to get a resounding affirmative. At least a dozen of those I spoke to were emphatic in their support. "It's hard to imagine this won't be a success," I remember one contact saying. The result of these careful conversations to gauge interest in me starting my own firm had an overwhelming conclusion: People didn't care what name was on the door as long as they continued to receive the high-quality service and research they had come to expect from Ivy Zelman.

I wanted my parting with Credit Suisse to be as amicable as possible, and so when I left in May of 2007, I didn't divulge that I was starting an independent research boutique. I kept where I was headed next vague, simply saying I had a lot of options—which was the truth. When Credit Suisse announced I had resigned, I received a flood of emails in the following weeks with job offers of all sorts. Some were soft inquiries; "What are you up to? Do you want to talk?" Others were very specific job offers, such as the number of private equity funds who invited me to work for them. Even Credit Suisse got in on the action, asking me to consider starting a fund that would be under their umbrella to invest in housing companies and stocks. I gave everyone the impression I needed time to decide my next step.

"Thank you," I said, "I'll be in touch."

The nonsolicitation clause in my contract with Credit Suisse lasted for sixty days and the noncompete clause for six months. Those terms precluded me from opening my doors until October 2007, and so we scheduled our launch for exactly six months from my departure date. It was certainly bold to leave the safety of my tenured job as a managing director at Credit Suisse to start my own firm in the teeth of the Great Recession. But it was my very boldness in making and sticking to my defining call on housing that enabled the entrepreneurial plunge in the first place; so, while somewhat crazy, it also felt right.

Because I had made sure to exit on the best terms possible, Credit Suisse wished me well and allowed me to take Malinda, Alan, and Dennis with me on my new journey. Our beloved T-shirt maker, Justin, moved to Houston with his wife, Mindy, and so wouldn't be joining the new venture. We parted friends and he went on to work for Invesco as a buy-side analyst for the next ten years before rejoining Zelman & Associates in 2018.

My industry movements became news. The *Wall Street Journal* even picked it up, giving us great visibility just when we needed it most and heralding a new future for the team. It was gratifying, being acknowledged for doing something brave by such an iconic publication. The first article in the *Journal* came when I announced I was leaving: "Credit Suisse Housing Expert Zelman Resigns," in which the author dubbed me a "blunt-speaking bearish analyst with a knack for spotting signs of trouble." The next came when we launched Zelman & Associates, "Expert on Housing has Her Own Nest: Zelman, Who Warned About Troubled Sector, Starts Research Firm." There on the page was a black-and-white pencil line drawing just like the *Journal* always does, but this time it was of me. My new reality was starting to sink in.

The Ivy who was fresh out of college, physically running to buy a *Journal* to frantically flip through before her Salomon interview, would have a hard time believing she was now among those same pages. I was proud to have accomplished something with my career that warranted not one, but two articles, in the *Wall Street Journal*. I was delighted to be the expert mainstream publications were quoting in discussions on the current recession in housing; (because, yes, the world had finally accepted the reality of the housing downtown). I was forty-one, and I felt I had arrived.

Four Unsung Heroes

I don't want to make it seem as if the decision to leave Credit Suisse was an easy one. I knew I wanted more and that I was ready to pull it off, but I received a lot of pushbacks. Most people thought I was out of my mind swapping a secure position with a high level of compensation for greater risk. Their concern hit with slightly more force when I considered that I had three young children at home, ages three, five, and seven at the time. But what those people didn't know, and what I reminded myself of, was that I had the hands-on support of loyal, caring, and intelligent people who I knew would have my back until the very end.

My husband, David, was essential to the founding of Zelman & Associates for a whole host of reasons. David is, and always has been, a very astute businessman—meaning, he was smart enough that he wasn't sure any of this was such a good idea. But he came around, like he always does. Plus, he was a great investor, providing us financial security.

"If you're committed to doing this," he said, "I'm all in."

He followed through on that promise and was extremely involved. He created the infrastructure for the entire back office. He secured our broker-dealer license. He ran sales. His support carried great weight; since the day we met at Salomon, he's been my most trusted adviser. Starting a business is significant and stressful and there were certainly times we didn't agree, but I have never doubted David's support was truly genuine. If I disagree with him on something with enough conviction, he will yield knowing he isn't going to win that battle. But over the years, David has confirmed time and time again he was a great counselor and a reliable voice of reason when I need it the most.

Kim Gray was another essential part of my support team. The office I had recently vacated in Ohio shared a wall with Michael Moses, a managing director in the real estate group at Credit Suisse. Our first meeting may have consisted of him berating me for playing Barney videos for my kids too loudly on one of their office visits, but we eventually became friends. Over time I took an interest in his assistant, Kim, who was a real dynamo. She was bursting with energy and seemed hungry for more. Eventually, Kim went to work for another company. A year later, we crossed paths once again. It was meant to be—the stars aligned! She wanted me to speak at an event and all I wanted was for her to work with me. I knew her passion and work ethic would further the values I wanted present in my new firm, so I offered her a job at my start-up.

Of course, Kim didn't jump at the chance right away; she was loyal to the company she was at, which made her an even more attractive hire. Eventually, however, I managed to convince her that she would be a valued and integral part of the great team I was building and she agreed to become my administrator in Cleveland.

Despite being based in another state for much of our relationship, Malinda had been a treasured companion since the day we met and was key to getting Zelman & Associates off the ground. Years earlier, Malinda was assigned to me by the head of the secretary pool at Salomon as my former secretary couldn't keep pace and was fired. When I was told my replacement had arrived, I rushed to find her as I was eager to get a feel for this person I'd be working so closely with. I found her at her desk, in a cubicle without walls, and I leaned over to say hello. She had her head down and was eating her breakfast. Slowly, she looked up and in a calm voice she said, "I will come find you when I'm done eating my breakfast." Her tone and her piercing brown eyes told me everything I needed to know; she was in charge. She was a woman with a long tenure on Wall Street, and I absorbed her wisdom with eagerness. I valued her input as I knew it was born of experience and was grateful to have her by my side.

Our bond deepened immediately, and Malinda soon became my anchor. I spoke to her nearly every day of my life since our first meeting in 1992. I gave her daily updates regarding issues with employees, salespeople, clients, and vented regularly about my personal life. Malinda listened in on many of my business calls and knew all my deepest secrets. In many ways, she felt like an extension of me, and I loved her dearly. We lost Malinda in November, 2020, when her heart suddenly gave out and she passed away at the young age of sixty-one. To this day, my first inclination when anything happens in my life, good or bad, is to call her. It fills me with pain each time my brain catches up and reminds me that she's gone. In some ways, though, I hope the urge to share with Malinda never goes away. It's a testament to the impact she's had on my life.

The fourth unsung hero is my younger sister, Ally. We were close from the very beginning. When I left New York for Virginia to be with Ian, leaving Ally was the hardest part of the transition. From childhood, we had been confidantes. And so, when she decided to quit her job in Minneapolis, I swooped in to convince her to move to Cleveland. I wanted her close to me again. Initially, she worked as a leasing agent for Jody and Eric Bell's family's apartment building. However, soon after our final child, Zia, was born our nanny, Carol, notified us that she wasn't up for handling three children at sixty years old. We came up with an arrangement where she would care for Zia, and Ally would come on board to watch Zach and Zoey. A few years later, Carol retired, and Ally became our full-time childcare and house manager. Her role was invaluable in affording me the time to focus on the firm and giving me the confidence I needed to travel or be otherwise occupied. I knew things would be handled, even when I was so deep in work, I couldn't afford a moment of attention elsewhere. But in addition to this logistical support, it was so special to be living life alongside my sister daily once more. She was and is truly my best friend and has lent me endless strength; I cannot count the times we have vented, cried, or laughed together.

Smiling and Dialing

Our initial team was split between two cities. In New York, Dennis, Alan, and Malinda moved into a shared office building in Midtown; while David, Kim, and I moved into a shared Regus office space in the suburbs of Cleveland. It was maybe two hundred square feet, barely big enough for one person, but we somehow managed to cram four desks in there. A good deal of shuffling took place every time someone attempted to leave the room, but it didn't bother me. I was thrilled we were out on our own.

We tackled things as they came. I suddenly found myself dealing with aspects of the business I never had to think about before: setting up medical insurance and other benefits for our employees, paying the utility bills, locating permanent office space, dealing with recruiting and hiring—even, to my chagrin, figuring out the process through which clients would remunerate us. I had never doubted we would have customers willing to pay, but I had also never thought through how they'd do so. Before long, I realized that I had expected to be able to transplant my exact business from Credit Suisse elsewhere, with my name on the door. There were elements of going out on my own, however, that I didn't expect or account for, and they popped up left, right, and center. David's sister, Darcy, ended up jumping in to help us handle the bookkeeping. We were in a jam, and she had the time and experience to help. Before long, her part-time involvement swelled to her becoming a full-time member of the team. She worked for us for years, until she passed away in 2015 following a long battle with cancer, leaving behind her three amazing children Sophie, Max, and Sadie who I cherish. We felt her loss acutely both in the business and, more important, in our family life.

For the six months before we could formally commence business, the team worked tirelessly to get our launch report finished while David focused on securing the broker-dealer license. Like his sister, my husband played a key role in helping me tackle the unexpected challenges that came with setting up the firm. He helped me deal with FINRA, the regulator that oversees broker-dealers, and navigate the complicated compliance considerations that are so crucial to get right. Somehow, two weeks after our non-solicitation agreement expired, we were ready for our first conference call to clients. The salesforce consisted of David and me. There we sat, squeezed into our tiny box of an office, smiling and dialing, getting people to come on board. Some of my Credit Suisse clients were not able to commit to an annual remuneration as their payment was determined by an internal vote after services had been rendered, but many gave us verbal commitments which, on Wall Street, was enough. By the time we hosted our first official Zelman call, we had signed up seventy-five clients. We were on our way.

It was during this phase that one of my clients asked, "What is the highest level of payment you're receiving?"

What he was really asking is: "How much do I have to pay for us to be the hedge fund that gets the first call?" Now, we'd never tell anyone anything ahead of anyone else; when we published a note, it went out to the whole distribution list, and everyone received the same insight at the same time. But immediately after that, everyone knew we'd be picking up the phone and calling our best clients one at a time. You might be wondering, how is that order determined?

Well, our clients knew: those who paid the most got the first call. Depending on their clout and size, certain players were willing to pay a premium to jump to the top of the list. They wanted to know that when they called, we'd drop everything to service them. If they said jump, we'd say, how high?

The gentleman on the phone asked again: "What is your top client paying you?"

I quoted him a figure that was a bit north of the truth, but close enough to be considered in the ballpark. He went 50 percent higher than that to secure his premier position. I hung up the phone and told David the news in what can only be described as a shriek. He stood up in his tight space and broke out into a dance which went on to become famous in the Zelman household and has been affectionately termed the "money dance." Pressure and excitement alike fueled our efforts. I'd wake up at 3:00 a.m., too invigorated to go back to sleep. It wasn't unusual for me to climb out of bed and start working long before the sun was up. We were on fire, and I couldn't get enough of it.

The palpable energy in the air those days also came from the dissolution of so many well-known companies, one falling quickly after another. Daily, we were waking up to the news of a fresh disaster. It was like watching one long, continuous train wreck. At the time of our launch, the worst to come hadn't yet taken place. We were only in the early to middle stages of what would go on to become the greatest recession the United States—and the world—had ever experienced.

Taking a page from the hedge funds' ability to see opportunities in distressed situations, we realized we needed to flesh out our team just as there was an influx of talented Wall Street professionals who were suddenly without work. The demise of Bear Stearns was particularly well-timed for us. In March 2008, JP Morgan bought Bear Stearns for $2 a share with the Federal Reserve promising to cover $30 billion of mortgage securities to get the deal done. We procured a list of the analysts and salespeople whose jobs would be in jeopardy and cold-called them to see if any would be interested in joining our start-up. Several former Bear Stearns employees joined us that year, including Michele Segalla, a senior salesperson who gave us seven incredible years before leaving to spend more time with her family; and Lauren Bome, who runs our marketing initiatives to this day. Ryan McKeveny, an undergraduate from Villanova who grew up in Rochester, New York, also came aboard around this time, bringing with him a willingness to work hard and wear many hats; over the ten years from his joining, I have watched him blossom from a reserved entry-level analyst to our senior analyst covering mortgage and real estate services who regularly presents to large companies with poise and confidence. And so it was that under the backdrop of relentless headlines announcing new corporate failures, the termination of CEOs, and megamergers intended to keep banks that were too big to fail from failing, our team swelled, and our research firm thrived. Housing was at the center of the crisis and our clients were depending on our guidance to navigate the storm.

Flipping the Script

Our first Zelman & Associates conference was held on the day that Lehman Brothers filed for Chapter 11 bankruptcy in September 2008. In a way, the juxtaposition was the perfect symbol for the founding of our company. We emerged from the ashes of extensive financial ruin to claim success. We are not the only company to have done this, of course. The history of Wall Street is full of organizations who innovated when faced with wreckage; but we were proud to join the ranks of those who didn't let fear stand in their way.

When we founded Zelman and, of course, had complete autonomy while designing our processes, we vowed that our conferences would be different from the standard fare. Typically, individual public companies present after a host introduces them, scrolling through PowerPoint slides on why attendees should invest in their stocks for thirty minutes before transitioning into a question-and-answer period. The Q&A is the best part; many attendees are there mainly to hear how management responds to the challenging questions they're faced with on the spot.

I wanted to take the best part of the existing model and expand on it, replacing the duller portions with content I thought would better inform and excite. Instead of static presentations, we put on a series of panels at our first housing summit which took place at the Four Seasons outside of Dallas. In addition to hosting publicly traded companies, we also pioneered the event by inviting private companies into the mix to get a wider range of insights. We had a great network of private firms, so why not share their experience which we were so fortunate to access? We offered clients the standard conference platform to meet with the public company management teams in one-on-one settings or small group meetings while the panels were in session, providing a convenient and valuable opportunity for investors to interact directly with important executives while we stood by to give our sought-after perspective when needed.

Dennis opened the proceedings with an in-depth, State of the Nation–style presentation on housing, which went on to become the most popular and highest attended portion of our events. Afterward, I moderated multiple panels comprised of both private and public CEOs from all silos of the industry, allowing for an in-depth discussion of the market that engaged and educated the audience.

I'm sure it comes as little surprise that as a moderator I didn't ask easy questions; I asked the questions that needed to be answered. At one such conference, our keynote speaker Dr. Michael Roizen, cofounder of RealAge and the former chief wellness officer at the Cleveland Clinic, stayed on to watch the panels after finishing his speech. He found me after the final event of the day to say in admiration: "You're unbelievable."

I tried to reciprocate the compliment and thank him for the impact he had on my attendees, but he doubled down.

"No, I mean it. You're talented."

"Talented at what?" I asked.

"It's rare to be able to moderate like that. You know how to interrupt, but in a nice way. You don't let people drone on. You lead the discussion firmly, but without putting words in anyone's mouth."

It was interesting to receive a compliment for something I considered second nature. If I wanted to direct my panelists politely to another subject, I would. If I needed to interrupt them when they consumed too much airtime, I would. I have always been aware of how valuable people's time is to them; each attendee made a point to be at my conference, and so I made a point to ensure it was worth every minute of their time. I knew I couldn't sit back when someone rambled on or veered wildly off topic. I would pursue the lines of questioning the audience was hungry for, and make sure they got their answers even if the panelists were occasionally less than thrilled at the lines of inquiry pursued. I'm not saying we were the first to do panels. But we were one of the first to host a conference that was exclusively panels with industry executives in attendance. Now, nearly fifteen years later, virtually all other conferences are also exclusively panel. We set the trend. That first year we had over two hundred participants; now, we host an average of six hundred attendees per year.

From its founding, our firm was in the news frequently speaking to the state of the market. While many searched for the housing bottom after the economy reached its trough in 2009, we remained negative and warned there was no bottom in sight for housing. We were right.

To this day, people say, "Zelman called the top of the market. Zelman called the bottom of the market."

But we're not a one-hit wonder. We've made a lot of calls between then and now. We have consistently brought investors thoughtful and comprehensive thematic research that is forward-looking, and it nearly always comes to fruition. We strive to continuously meet their high expectations.

We have built a network of nearly one thousand companies that are partners with Zelman & Associates. I recently saw one of our clients speaking about her experience working with us on a video, and it simply and powerfully summed up the driving aim of our firm:

"Zelman is continuously coming out with thematic research that is ahead of the curve. Their information is predictive, current, and actionable. If you want to make wise decisions based on what the market is going to look like in two to three years . . . you can't get a deeper level of insight."

In addition to our impressive external network, I'm intensely proud of the culture we cultivated in-house at Zelman. Once someone joins the team, they're likely to stick around for a long time, if not become a lifer. Take Steve Wank our CFO and head of compliance, as well as Pete Carroll and Pam Scher, two of our tenured salespeople, who joined us over a decade ago. They are trusted professionals who are part of my family. We have newer additions including Ted Tabasso, Jeff Peters in sales, and Kevin Kaczmarek in research, who know that they matter, their life partners matter, their kids matter, and their work/life balance matters. Everyone is treated with respect and given autonomy and a great deal of responsibility early on in their time with us. I'd have new hires doing what a senior analyst does early in their careers, with the necessary training and support in place to ensure their success. I genuinely wanted, and still want, my team to learn, be independent, and grow under my leadership.

While the longevity of our employees is a testament to the power of the relational model we've adopted at Zelman, it's been further validated by how eager our team members have been to invite friends and family into the firm's fold. One such example is when Tony McGill, Dennis's brother, came on board. With his combined experience of having worked at Bear Stearns in capital markets and his studies at Oxford University, he brought big ideas to the table. Because of the welcoming environment at Zelman, Dennis and Tony both knew he was more than welcome to share his vision with me.

"You have an unbelievable Rolodex chock-full of owners and operators," he said. "You should be doing investment banking."

I didn't want to; I wasn't a fan of investment bankers and wasn't interested in expanding into that world. However, I knew Tony was humble and trustworthy, and I wanted to give him a chance and see what he could build. He didn't let me down; he put in hard, smart work and built an impressive investment banking business for Zelman.

There was also Jason Bernzweig, an analyst who had previously worked for me at Credit Suisse. Several years after I left to start my own firm, he reached out to suggest that David and I start a hedge fund. Before long, Jason had moved his family to Cleveland so that he and David could give it their best shot. After six years and about $300 million raised, they decided to end the hedge fund and return the money. They had done well, but they didn't fit the box required by institutional investors who wanted consistent returns as opposed to the fluctuating 30 percent to 70 percent returns, they were generating. By that point, they had had a great ride, but neither Jason nor David enjoyed it anymore and so they called it quits. Jason left to work at Impala, one of our best clients, and David transitioned into private investing for our family.

From the moment I first had the idea to launch my own firm, I knew it was important to me that I build a personal relationship with everyone who joined my team. I wanted each person who worked for me to know they were valued as a human being and as a friend. I wanted to create a space where they felt nurtured, challenged, and supported. My employees have never been and will never be just employees to me. And, while it has never been the point, the emphasis I place on treating people well has always seemed to pay dividends.

Chapter Ten

LOSE SOME
(BUT WIN MORE)

"That's one hell of a swing!"

While speaking about my experience of surviving breast cancer, I almost always include my love of golf. Those may seem like strange topics to associate, but everything in our lives is interconnected—a fact I grew to appreciate deeply during that time of my life.

I learned how to play golf when I was ten years old. I was the athlete of the family and so my dad started taking me with him to the driving range, before he quickly promoted me to the course to play a full round. He said I was a natural; actually, I believe his exact words were, "That's one hell of a swing!" As a kid, the fact that knowing how to golf would get me ahead in the business world was far from my mind. All I knew then was that it was fun, and I liked spending the time with my dad.

Yet despite loving the sport, I stopped playing golf as a teenager. I was distracted by normal things like boys and friendships, and some less common ones, like adjusting to living in the suburbs of London after my family's sudden move across the Atlantic. But fast-forward a decade or so and I was ready to get back into it. At twenty-seven, I was just starting out as a stand-alone sell-side analyst, and I had already realized that golf was offered on the boondoggles to which I was now being invited at a rapidly increasing rate. I called up my dad who was then living in Houston—the city where he would meet his current wife, Maryann, and asked me to stand as his best man at their wedding in August of 1983—to tell him I needed some more of his top-shelf golf lessons. I asked him to help me get new clubs and take me out again to refresh my skills.

My dad was thrilled his protégé was coming back. He was a golf fanatic; if he wasn't out on the course, he was watching videos or reading books to improve his game. After he walked me through the process of getting outfitted with new clubs, we headed straight to the driving range. I took a few swings and he turned to me with a broad grin on his face.

"You've still got it," he said.

We made plans to play a round the next day. I bounded down the stairs of his house in the morning, announcing that I was ready to go. My dad took one look at me and asked, "Where are you going?"

"We are going to play golf, right?"

"Well, yeah, I thought so. But you definitely can't go to the golf course dressed like that!"

I glanced down at my purple sports bra and matching biker shorts. I was a busy lady; if I was going to spend a day outside, I wanted to get some color at the same time. Of course, I didn't understand golf etiquette—you can't walk around the course half naked. I changed into something more appropriate and we were off, but that near faux pas is something he teases me about to this day.

I had been able to drive the ball more than two hundred yards straight down the driving range the day before, and so my dad was confident I was ready to play. I took pride in that swing. When a woman showed up on the course, certain men would make it clear they expected her to slow down their game or, even worse if they were paired up, that it would

148

take too long to complete a round of eighteen holes. Those assumptions changed the second they saw how I could drive the ball straight down the fairway. I loved watching their faces when that happened. Laura and I would lug our clubs, jumping on the number 4/5 train to play golf in the Bronx. The line of men waiting to play golf was initimidating but we showed them. When we got on the tee box and whacked the ball, we saw many of these annoyed mens' jaws drop, which was fun. However, I was never a great scorer and I was rarely consistent for eighteen holes, but I had a mean drive and a okay short game which were more than enough.

Golf became a big part of my life as an equity analyst; it was great for cementing relationships with management teams and, honestly, a handy way to impress clients.

Conversations unfolded differently on the course than they would have in a conference room. When you're on an outing that lasts four to six hours, conversation naturally extends beyond business concerns, even when playing with CEOs or other executives. It's also just a fun way to get to know people. The competitive element is, somewhat ironically, a great equalizer. It doesn't matter what your position is within a company—if you hit a ball and it's a duff, people are going to make fun of you.

I always thought of my penchant for golf as something of a secret weapon, but a colleague of mine recently told me: "I was just encouraging my daughter to learn to play golf because I saw how much it helped your career." So, apparently, it was more of an obvious asset than I realized.

While it doesn't have to be golf specifically, it is beneficial to be aware of the leisure activities that are most common in your field. Developing skills that create opportunities to engage with industry executives or clients in your sector is a worthwhile effort. I always felt lucky that a thing I loved and a thing I was good at also happened to be the best hobby possible to advance my career. I had it easy; until, that is, I had to give it all up as a result of cancer.

No Clean Margins

I went in for a routine mammogram—I think it was my second ever—and the moment the door of the doctor's office swung shut behind me, the experience had been forgotten. I had a business to run.

It was two weeks later that I looked up from where I was sitting at my desk to see my husband looking across the room at me with a serious expression on his face. He gestured me over.

You know it's not going to be something good that's coming when you're gently told, "Sit down."

David was holding a letter from the OBGYN office. Kim had come across it while sorting through our mail as she always did, and she figured she wasn't the right person to hand it to me. That's how it fell on my husband to inform me that something suspicious had been found on my breast and the doctor wanted me to come back in for a biopsy. He had hardly finished relaying the contents of the letter before he switched to reassurance mode.

"Don't get ahead of yourself, now. Everything could very well be fine . . ."

I told him I was okay, and honestly, at that point I wasn't particularly worried. I went in for the biopsy a few days later and the situation once again faded from my mind. I wasn't even sure how long it'd be until the results came in. It was that weekend, at Sunday dinner at my in-laws' house that I saw I had a voicemail from the doctor. *A call on a Sunday?* A tiny voice in my head whispered, *That's not a good sign.* I quietly retreated halfway up the staircase and sat down to call the doctor back. She got to the point quickly.

"Unfortunately, you do have cancer. But it's DCIS cancer, which is the least invasive kind. All you'll need to do is get a lumpectomy and that will be it. You will be fine after this, I'm sure."

At the time, I had no reason to doubt her. I pulled David aside and calmly filled him in. It was November of 2008 and I was forty-two years old. I had no idea that I was about to embark on a thirteen-year nightmare.

After a cancer surgeon performed the lumpectomy, the pathology showed I did not have clean margins. This meant the cancer was still present around the edges of their previous excision and they were going to need to do another lumpectomy. It was suggested more than it was explicitly said that if there weren't clean margins this time around, I'd be facing another level of concern entirely.

Because it was my second lumpectomy, I knew now how long it would take for the results to come in. I was flying home from a business trip the day I expected to hear the news. I called my sister after I landed, on the drive home from the airport.

"Has there been any word from the doctor?" I asked.

It's so hard—impossible, really—for sisters to keep anything from each other. There was a long pause, and then Ally dissolved into tears. "Yes, and I'm not supposed to tell you."

"You have to!"

"No, really, I can't. David will be so upset."

But eventually, she relented. There were no clean margins, she said. The doctor was recommending a mastectomy. I hung up the phone and was swallowed into the silence of the car.

Before she had folded, Ally tearfully explained that David was waiting to tell me about the results in person. He didn't want to upset me during my business meetings or have me come unglued in front of the kids, who were four, six, and eight at the time. I appreciated his thought process and wanted to join him in his efforts to keep everything calm. As I pulled into our driveway, I mustered all my self-control. I focused on each step: getting out of the car, going into the house, kissing my kids, and greeting my dogs. The entire time *I'm going to get a mastectomy* played on loop in my head. The words didn't feel real. We sat down to dinner as a family. Every night, whether it's just David and me, all five of us, or even when we're hosting guests, we go around the table and each person shares our favorite part of the day and something we're grateful for. This is a tradition I treasure, but that night I found it hard to speak around the hard lump in my throat.

When the kids finally went to bed, David sat me down and told me the pathology results. I wanted to make it easier for him, so I pretended to be hearing the news for the first time. I went to bed still feeling numb. It wasn't until I bolted upright in the middle of the night that the emotions started to hit me, chief among them overwhelming despair. My response surprised me. I climbed out of bed and made my way to the kitchen table where I started writing a letter to my mother, my go-to for all things medical. The words came pouring out of me as reality set in that I was going to lose my breast, part of my womanhood. There at the table at three o'clock in the morning, I put onto the paper everything that I couldn't or shouldn't say to my immediate family who needed me to be strong.

Among the 5 percent

Even though the cancer only seemed to be present in one breast, my doctors recommended that I do a double mastectomy. If I went that route, I was told there was a 95 percent chance I'd be done with cancer forever. And ultimately, that was the goal; I was most concerned with coming out of the operating room without any cancer left in my body. It's difficult to convey what a difficult choice that was, or how it feels to mutilate your own body, but it felt worth taking such a drastic step knowing there was just a 5 percent chance I would still have cancer afterward.

By this point, you should know the drill; I was among the 5 percent. After the operation, the pathology report showed I still had cancer in some of the remaining tissues in my body. The doctors recommended seven weeks of radiation, with five sessions per week. That may well have been the hardest season of my life. As draining as it was physically, it was the loneliness that most wore on me. No matter how many people loved me and wanted to be there for me, no one was allowed to accompany me into the cold room where I sat under a hovering machine, day in and day out. My bilateral mastectomy was meant to be my ticket back to normalcy, and the cost had been steep. I spent much of my time in that cold radiation room wondering how it was that I paid the price yet still ended up in this position?

When I finished my seven weeks of radiation, the doctors were hopeful the cancer was gone but there was no way of really knowing. All we could do was wait. My life had been dramatically disrupted for months already, and my health issues would drag on for years to come, including the issues I had with my implants that sent me back to the hospital several times over. I was forced to cancel my normal business travel for marketing and company meetings. My cancer didn't seem to care that we were in the early parts of the housing recovery, or that all my hard work was starting to pay off. I wanted to be able to take advantage of the many opportunities for significant exposure that came my way. I was called to testify in front of the U.S. Senate, which I was fortunately able to do, but there were many other invitations I was forced to pass on, such as speaking to the executive board of Fannie Mae. I was grateful to have Dennis to send in my place, but it was devastating to be sidelined during what felt like the peak of my career.

From my first year of college, I had been forging an ironclad work ethic. Giving my very best to my work had become a foundational part of my identity and it was a dizzying adjustment to no longer be able to run my business the way I wanted or needed to. But even as I struggled to process the change in the professional sphere of my life, I came to accept the need to focus on my recovery. As part of that process, I learned how to truly rely on the incredible team of people around me for the first time in my life.

David, Ally, Malinda, Kim, and a host of my girlfriends supported me during those long months, leaving an impact that will never be forgotten. They were there to bring me lunch, make sure I took my medicine, lay next to me in bed, hold me in their arms, and cry with me on the hardest days. These acts of kindness made my closest friends angels in my eyes.

My mother came to stay with me while I was recovering from one of my surgeries. She not only helped take care of me physically but also did her best to distract me from the misery that threatened to overwhelm me. Given my general unwillingness to leave my room at the time, her options were limited. One day, she decided I wasn't treating my designer purses well enough. They were flopped over one another on the floor of my closet. She looked over at me slumped in bed.

"Alright," she said. "Today, we are going to figure out a way to get these purses to stand up nice and straight."

For the next hour, my mother and I took random items from David's side of the closet and stuffed them into the bags. I was on painkillers at the time, so the memory didn't come back to me in full clarity until years later when I opened one of those purses and pulled out old rolled up T-shirts and sweatshirts of David's. I remember laughing with my mother when I had stuck them in there, and I called her then to laugh about it some more.

I'm not sure how to fully convey how hard this period was on me and my family. I went in for the routine mammogram in November of 2008. My final surgery occurred in July, 2021. For years, most areas of my life came to a screeching halt as I dealt with operation after operation and near constant pain. As the end of my misery finally seemed to be nearing, my doctors cautioned that I might experience some difficulty with certain physical activities at first, like playing golf, but assured me that physical therapy would help get me close to my precancer performance levels. If I wasn't trying to compete on a professional level, they said, I could go back to swimming, skiing, and golfing. Unfortunately, but perhaps unsurprisingly, they were wrong. No matter how hard I tried to build the muscles in my back that were impacted by my later surgeries, I have yet to take more than a few swings of my club without experiencing bouts of severe pain afterward. But I haven't given up; I continue to do strength training with the hope that golf will again be part of my life someday.

While the cost climbed higher than I could have ever imagined at the beginning of the ordeal, I finally got what I was after: a clean bill of health, as far as cancer is concerned. Over the course of those years, I developed deep humility and empathy for others going through medical struggles of their own which have never left me. And, while opting for the double mastectomy caused me several grave medical issues down the line, I do not regret the decision. It is a choice that allowed me to show my family they were—and are—my priority, and one that gave me the chance to jump fully back into the life I had so missed living.

Chapter Eleven

MAKE PEOPLE A PRIORITY
(GAL PALS CAN SAVE YOUR LIFE)

"I am true to my name;
once Ivy grows on something, you can't get rid of it."

While my experience with cancer drove the point home, I had long ago identified the immense value good friendships bring into my life. It may be easy to point to female friendships as an essential ingredient to my emotional well-being, but it takes hard work to maintain them. When I click with someone, it feels like falling in love. In a moment, I know the two of us are meant to be friends. From then, I am true to my name; once Ivy grows on something, you can't get rid of it. I'm yours forever, and I will put concerted and sustained effort into nourishing our relationship.

My friends and I make sure to show up for each other's big moments, of course, but we've also learned the art of sharing daily life even from afar. Not a day goes by without at least one phone call from a girlfriend, my sister Ally included. They aren't always deep, meaningful heart-to-hearts. Our conversations range from *I just had a huge fight with my husband* to *I just watched the best new show*, and everything in between. Sometimes, we talk about absolutely nothing; I'll hang up the phone after an hour-long call with Jennifer and I couldn't tell you a single substantive thing that was said. Maybe we discussed the shows we're watching, the color we got our nails painted, or our step count for the day. Jennifer is a newer friend that I met fifteen years ago when our oldest children became friends in kindergarten. Kyle and Zoey were inseparable and so we became friends. Because she is a working mother and a strong woman, we bonded immediately and have been together ever since. Our daily conversations may seem pointless at times, but they matter. Little by little, they build the foundation for the support we can offer one other when times get tough—as they invariably do.

We also get to weather the aging process together, which is huge. Aging affects everything from our physical health to our self-esteem. We're getting wrinkles. Our hair is thinning. We have cellulite. To be frank, it sucks, but having friends going through it at the same time makes all the difference. I might not talk to a certain friend for a whole week when I get a text:

"Are you still taking iron as one of your vitamins?"

"Yes."

"Send me a picture of the brand you're using."

It's nice to have each other to discuss which products we should be using to make our skin look better and what vitamins are best for staying healthy. Or to gossip with when there's a scandal in our wider community. Or to discuss the masterpiece Anna Quindlen published, *Lots of Candles, Plenty of Cake*, which is about finding joy and balance in what is the inevitable process of aging.

Or even to share the silly rays of hope, like when Yvette called excitedly to say, "A guy just checked me out at the gas station!"

"Like the attendant?" I asked.

"No, you dumbass, a hot guy in a Mercedes."

"Oh my God, tell me the story!" I want to hear every detail. Yvette and I have been best friends since we were thirteen years old. She was my partner in crime in my teens, right there by my side as we talked our way backstage at rock concerts. When we were young, we would stride into bars side by side. We knew there were many sets of eyes trailing us through the room and we relished in it. But when you're over fifty and people rarely notice you, you must celebrate the small victories. Yvette lives in Westport, Connecticut, so I get to see her more often than some of my other wonderful friends. She is a prolific reader always providing me political updates and breaking news. We have traveled to London, Paris, Switzerland, and Amsterdam together and are currently planning a trip to Dublin, Ireland. She is usually in charge of arranging our travel plans which I'm grateful for.

Sometimes a friend simply reaches out with a happy memory.

"Remember bouncing on Lori's bed to 'Only the Good Die Young?'" Yvette might ask. Or Maria will send a text saying, "I just watched a movie about cowboys and it made me think about the weekend in Phoenix we went horseback riding with those guys. Remember that?"

With several of these women, there are decades upon decades of memories. For example, Peggy Hurley, who I first met more than thirty-five years ago, and who now lives in Maryland with her husband, Hardy, and her son, Nate, always seems to make her way to Cleveland to celebrate every milestone event important to me and my family. Wendy Carroll was my first true friend. We grew up on Long Island together and attended the same school from kindergarten through to seventh grade. However, our hobbies did not indicate that we were little girls; we played backgammon, gambled, and sneaked cigarettes late into the night when we were far too young to be smoking.

Then there's Doreen. With her, the memories stretch back over forty years. I met her when I was ten years old and she was twelve. While

Doreen was my sister Caryn's age, we all hung out, including her younger sister Tracy. Doreen and I often reminisce about the days after high school when we were both living in New York City and both struggling. She had a walk-up in Greenwich Village on Leroy Street while I was on the Upper East Side. Doreen was my rabbi then, teaching me how to stick up for myself and also showing me how to enjoy what the lower part of NYC had to offer. She did all this while going to night school at NYU and working at a bank full-time. While she is now out on Long Island with her two sons and husband, we've remained surprisingly similar: protecting our families, supporting one another, and having a good time.

While we enjoy strolling down memory lane, we're committed to making time for new experiences as well. As often as we can, we schedule special girls' trips to celebrate our years of friendship and invest in one another away from the hustle and bustle of work and family obligations. The primary objective is to relax; we shop, sightsee, drink wine, laugh. On these trips, women who had never met but were brought together through knowing me emerge as partners in crime.

There have been times in my life when shit really hit the fan that I cannot imagine having endured without a friend by my side. When Ian and I split up after five years together and he moved out of the home we shared, I found myself alone and devastated. Maria moved in without hesitation. She even slept in my bed to comfort me during the transition period as I adjusted to my new normal. Within a few weeks, I could see that Ian and I had been drifting apart for some time, and that the breakup was for the best. Ian and I are still great friends and I love his wife, Manon. They live in Montreal and have participated in many of my family's milestones, including Bat and Bar Mitzvahs and my fiftieth birthday party. We laugh about old times and catch up on current events in our lives, forever bonded—I love Ian with all my heart.

Back in 1989, with Ian and I no longer together, I was able to get back on track, this time with an even clearer view of what I needed to do to be successful. I have no doubt my healing process would have taken infinitely longer without a key girlfriend showing up and having my back like Maria did. Maria still lives in Northern Virginia with her husband and two daughters but when we get on the phone it's as if we are still nineteen years old talking about our families, the latest TV series we both love, or challenges we are facing. I'm so blessed to have these amazing women in my life.

Good friends not only support you but also are there for your entire family. My friend, Jody, who I met through David's crew before we got married, lost her oldest son, Griffin, in an inexplicable tragedy. He was only twenty-five years old, and his passing absolutely broke her heart. I tried not to let a day go by without calling her then; even if she didn't feel like talking, I wanted her to hear my voice on the other end of that line and know that someone saw her pain and cared that she was hurting. Sometimes, I'd even be able to make her laugh. My life is in constant chaos, so I'd distract her with my best rendition of some silly woe from my day. When you're there for someone in a crisis, when you're willing to step outside of your own life to help them deal with theirs, you're creating an ironclad bond. When I was in surgery getting my mastectomy, it was Jody who sat with my husband for six hours straight telling him it was going to be okay.

On September 11, 2001, my flight from Cleveland to Chicago was grounded in Toledo. Leisa, my bestie since we met in England in eighth grade and who lives in Salt Lake City with her three daughters and six grandchildren, remembered I was flying that day and called David to tell him to turn on the news since she knew we didn't usually watch television in the mornings. Because I had a circle of women out there who truly had my back, David was made aware of what was going on and told me to get off that plane and take a taxi home from Toledo. A decade later, Leisa was another of the dear friends who flew clear across the country to be with me after one of my cancer surgeries and joins us on all the European girl trips, a constant presence in my life.

Do Unto Others

I've had people say to me: "You're so lucky to have so many great friends," when really, there's no luck involved. It takes effort and focus to make sure you're showing up for someone else in a real way. I've realized it's not just about being considerate and remembering anniversaries and birthdays, but rather doing everything I can to make sure my friends know I'm on their side and that I'll be there when they need me.

That said, there have certainly been times in my life I wish I had been a better friend, especially back when I was working eighty hours a week. Leisa was the first person in my circle who got divorced. Because she lives in Utah and I didn't see her challenges up close, I don't think I appreciated the struggle she went through raising three young children by herself. By the time I had three kids of my own under the age of six, I realized how amazing she truly was. While I wish I had been more available to Leisa back then, I know I can't rewrite the past. What I can do is be the best friend possible now and into the future.

I try to teach this to my kids; it can't always be about you. You have to be available when people need you. It's not just about hanging out when the good times are rolling. Being a great listener is a huge component of most, if not all, of the long-term friendships I have. I tell my children to ask their friends good questions and then to truly listen to their answers, even when they don't have any advice to offer.

Fortunately, they have the benefit of seeing the same prioritization of friendship exemplified by their father as well. David has friendships spanning back as far as preschool, with many members of his childhood friend group opting to attend Ohio State. When he moved back to Cleveland, they were able to pick back up right where they had left off. Even from afar, David had maintained those relationships and now, back in Cleveland, he sees his boys on a regular basis for Buckeye games, concerts, or just to hang out.

A beautiful element of friendships is that they sometimes spring from surprising places. Take my friend, Sherry, for example. We attended the same school for six weeks in seventh grade, before my family moved to England. Somehow, that was enough for a friendship to blossom, and we have sustained that relationship to this day. I have also found unexpected friendship in my daily routine with my Pilates instructor, Raudel; my trainer, Raul; my nail technician, Anna; my massage therapist, Victor; my hairdresser, Lisa; and my hair stylist, Luciano. Additionally, I have grown a deep bond with Annelise and Austin, a young married couple who manage my household and are enthusiastic real estate investors; they eagerly soak up the housing knowledge I share with them while also caring for me and my family. I have grown to love each of these people and consider myself lucky to have them in my life.

I have old friends like Laura, who helped me prepare for the morning calls at Salomon. I have new friends like Jennifer whose family has become intermeshed with my own. She played a key role in making Cleveland feel like home; there are so many parallels in the lives we're leading, and I treasure our daily check-ins. I have friends down the street, like Stacey, a brilliant and ball-busting OBGYN who joins me on long walks with our dogs. I have friends overseas like Elena, who lives on the island of Cyprus and yet we still manage to talk consistently, FaceTime, and plan meetups around the world. I treasure each one of these unique women. Their unconditional love, intelligence, and support make me stronger in a way I could never quantify. Friendships are truly the glue that holds my life together.

Chapter Twelve

GO UPSTAIRS
(YES, IT'S A STRUGGLE TO DO IT ALL)

"Mom, it's okay. I understand."

Early in my career, I was so focused on being successful that I rarely focused on my personal life. Finance was my passion to the point I wasn't sure if I had space in my life for kids. Once my children arrived, however, I realized nothing in the world mattered to me as much as them. I would literally cut off my right arm to help or protect Zoey, Zach, and Zia. While realizing where my heart's true mission lay was a beautiful moment in my life, I still struggled to find the proper balance between being an excellent mother and being a leader in my industry.

First, a warning: as a woman, you will almost surely receive unsolicited advice from men who have strong opinions on working moms. I like to refer to this group of men as assholes. Once, the chief investment officer of a hedge fund I had just met noticed I was heavily pregnant. I had barely finished saying, "It's nice to meet you," when he barked, "When are you due?" I told him my due date was in two months, but that this was my third baby, so I was a pregnancy pro at this point. He didn't crack a smile.

"You should be home with your children, not here with me," he said.

The way he said it was icy. There was such judgment in his voice. I knew this asshole's opinion wasn't worth anything, but it was a devastating interaction, nonetheless. Unfortunately, this story is not some wild exception. Every day, similar exchanges take place in the lives of professional women across the globe. What should be done in those situations? Are we supposed to pretend we didn't hear the rude commentary and continue to make small talk? Maybe, sometimes. But as a working mother, it's crucial to acknowledge society's double standard as part of your efforts to stay sane and retain confidence in your decisions.

The truth is that both women *and* men have to figure out how to marry their thirst for success with their desire to be a strong, present parent. For most of us, this is a process and not something that clicks into place automatically. I had to learn how not to plan a business trip when one of my three children was performing in a concert or a play or competing in a sporting event. I was used to thinking about the needs of my business. Like many driven individuals, I thought my personal life was where the sacrifices could be made. I can identify the specific day that erroneous belief was shattered.

I was in a taxi bound for LaGuardia Airport where I was meant to catch a flight home, but we were stuck in gridlocked traffic on Grand Central Parkway in Queens. It began to sink in that I was very likely going to miss my flight. When I finally made my way through security, I took off for my gate at a run even though I was in the second trimester of my pregnancy with Zach, my son. I got to the gate in time to see the flight attendant shut the door to the gangway. I grabbed her arm, my hands slick from sweat, "Please," I croaked, "I'm on that flight."

She said there was nothing she could do. I stood at the wide windows overlooking the tarmac and I cried. I knew it would be hours more before I got home now, if I was even able to get home that same night at all. My oldest daughter, Zoey, would fall asleep wondering why her mommy hadn't been there to tuck her in when she had promised over and over that she would be.

I'm not saying I turned into a stereotypical soccer or dance mom, but I moved a solid step closer to finding the balance that was right for my family. I decided I would be the mother who is at everything she can possibly be at, but if something arose that demanded my attention and was crucial to my career, I would attend to it—and I would try to do so without guilt, which never really worked.

Trying to establish a work/life balance sometimes means you don't fit in with the other moms. That was never more evident for me than when Zoey moved from recreational to competitive dance. I didn't sit around the table hand-sewing costumes or stay to chat for the girls' whole three-hour practice, which incited their judgmental stares. But I was there at every recital, making sure Zoey's makeup was on and standing in the wings to assist with costume changes, and then later when Zia became a competitive dancer.

Getting the balance right seemed to hinge on finding more ways to be present and contribute to my children's daily lives. I started working from home more often so I could be there when they got off the bus, for example. This generally went well, but it wasn't always smooth. It's hard for a kid to understand that yes, Mom is home, but no, she's not available now. Sometimes I could keep them at bay with a firm hand up and serious glare. Other times, when Zia would come in bawling her eyes out because Zach supposedly smacked her over the head with a board game, I would kindly request my work colleague to hold while I calmed the yelling the waiting party could surely hear.

Daily family dinners became an essential part of our household; sitting down to eat with the whole family was a tradition David grew up with, but one I had only occasionally experienced. These dinners presented an opportunity to instill some discipline in the kids. They took turns setting and clearing the table, loading the dishwasher, or scrubbing the pots and pans; they had to sit up straight and hold their forks correctly and, like all kids, I'm sure they appreciated the sense of predictability these expectations communicated even if they sometimes complained. But, most important, family dinners were a special time to be close as a family and share what was going on in each of our lives.

Going Upstairs

My favorite Zelman family ritual, one I treasure even more than family dinner, is what we call "going upstairs." Going upstairs has looked different in each phase of our children's lives. When they were little, David and I would go upstairs to monitor bath time or teeth brushing before we got into the good stuff: the reading and singing rotations. The kids would snuggle in bed as we read them *Goodnight Moon* or *Oh the Places You'll Go.* We had a rotation of favorite songs: "Memories," "Sun Rise Sun Set," "Somewhere Over the Rainbow," and "Puff the Magic Dragon" (which always made me cry). It brings joy to my heart that my three children will think of me whenever they hear any of those songs. Even on days David and I were exhausted and drained, and would rather have quiet time to ourselves, we went upstairs no matter what. And I was always glad I did; those sleepy moments before bedtime were the best part of my day.

As the kids aged, the routines shifted but the commitment stayed the same. I continued to go upstairs, but now it was to hang out and give them a chance to open up to me. They might tell me about school stress, friend drama, or their newest crush. Gone were the days of overseeing their bedtime routines; rather, my youngest, Zia, took to coming in and sitting with me as I took off my makeup and underwent my prebedtime ritual. While she played with her bestie, our Australian shepherd Zilli, she'd chat about what was going on with her life; sometimes it was light and silly, but sometimes she really opened to me and we had true heart-to-hearts.

Zia and I have always had a special connection regarding animals. From the time she was a toddler, it was clear to me that the two of us were in sync. I remember taking my children to see the movie *Marley & Me* many years ago. Halfway through, Zach and Zoey were bored and ready to go. But Zia, at just three years old, was sitting on my lap absolutely enthralled by what was happening on screen. By the end of the film, she was bawling right along with me. She had totally tracked with the storyline, and it had touched her. The similarity in the manner and depth that we both feel things has held strong throughout the years.

As they crept ever closer to college age, I treasured each moment I spent sitting with the kids in their childhood bedrooms. Sometimes, one of them and I would go on a tear and crack each other up; that was the best because, if it seemed like someone was having too much fun, the other kids would drift in to make sure they didn't miss out. The nights that this happened are among some of my happiest memories.

While I am nostalgic for the days of their childhood, I enjoy my relationships with my children in new, but equally fierce ways now that they're older. Zoey, my eldest, calls me nearly every day. She is relentlessly chipper, and I look forward to hearing her happy voice. As a kid, Zoey possessed a wisdom beyond her years. While Zach and Zia would melt down every time I left on a business trip, Zoey would look me in the eye and say, "Mom, it's okay. I understand." It made it all the better when I was able to take her along with me to New York, where we'd get our nails done, go to Bloomingdale's with Malinda, and catch a show on Broadway. Now, so many years later, it means an immense deal to me that she chooses to reach out every day, even as she is busy having fun and creating a new life for herself at college.

I've had friends say to me that they can't believe how much my kids tell me, even now, but I purposefully established and maintained an open dialogue with them from a very young age. I share about myself, both my ups and downs professionally and personally, and they're willing to respond in kind. I really don't think they hold much back. They know I am their confidante, a safe place.

Hitting the Road

It is important that I spend time with each of the children individually, so they feel seen and valued. We might catch a play, go out for dinner, or shop 'til we drop—a hobby I picked up from my own mother that I was more than happy to pass along to the next generation. Sometimes, I'd tie the quality time to my work. I wanted my children to get a taste of the business world and see their mother in action. I think it's beneficial for children to see a parent working, accomplishing goals, and forging a path in the world—whether a man or a woman. I believe they absorb, as if by osmosis, certain lessons about how to conduct themselves and what goes into success.

To help combat the sadness I felt leaving my kids for business trips, I came up with the idea of writing in journals for each of them. Every time I prepared to head out of town, I would put some thoughts down in the designated journal I bought for each of the three of them. In fact, I was so superstitious I wouldn't get on a plane without writing to them first, but while they know they exist they haven't read any of them. I just gave Zoey her books for her twenty-first birthday. I was surprised by how emotional we both became reading about us playing peek-a-boo while she was in her crib and so much more. Zach and Zia will have to wait until they turn the same age. Zach said he will need to hire someone to decipher my chicken scratch, which I laugh at.

But once the kids were old enough, I occasionally took one of them with me on my business trips on a rotating basis when I could. Each day, there'd be some bargaining. I'd promise we'll go do something fun that you like to do if you just let me finish my speech first. I remember bringing Zach along to a mortgage conference in Dallas when he was only eight years old. I had dressed him up in a suit and tie and told him that if he sat patiently while I gave my speech, we'd go swimming at the hotel pool after. The second I got off stage, Zach was ready to go. But Ed DeMarco, the director of the FHFA, the federal agency established to oversee Fannie Mae and Freddie Mac, stepped up to speak next.

"Zach, we can't leave yet," I said, "It's really important I hear what this man has to say."

I wanted to say hello to Ed after his speech concluded, but there were a whole bunch of people trying to do the same. Too many people don't use this valuable opportunity to chat with great speakers after they present. You need to be assertive and willingly put yourself out there. Separately, and understandably, Zach was growing increasingly annoyed. For the third time, I told my son he'd have to wait.

"But I'll tell you what," I said, "here are some business cards. Go around and swap these with other people, okay? Get theirs in return for mine." I just wanted to keep him busy.

Nearly fifteen minutes later, I still hadn't spoken to Ed. I went to hand the gentleman I was standing next to my business card while we waited together, and he laughed.

"I actually already got one of those from your son. Look at him go!"

I turned around to see my eight-year-old son working the room, weaving between rows of desks where I could have never fit and handing a card to every person he saw. I burst out laughing.

During these trips, and at dinner at home on a regular basis, I would discuss my business with my kids. It wasn't something I did intentionally, but it naturally came up given the activities and conversations they were surrounded by. The kids took to asking, "Were the stocks green or red today, Mom?"

I remember an evening when we were having leftover lamb stew for dinner. Zach took one look at his bowl and said, "I don't want to eat this."

"Just eat it," David said. "It costs money."

"But, Dad, it's a sunk cost," he answered.

Zach was twelve years old. David blinked back at him like, *How the hell do you know that?*

We shouldn't necessarily have been surprised though. This was the same child who, at middle-school summer camp, found himself in a somewhat serious conversation about the economy with a few other boys. There was one loud-mouthed kid drowning everyone else's thoughts out. Zach shut him up in one fell swoop: "Okay, so what's your source?" I was bursting with both laughter and pride when I heard the story.

Family dinners often featured lively discussions about the stock market, politics, and current events. I was delighted to find that my kids can dig; they could be convincing, even charismatic, challenging David and me with their knowledge. As they got older, it wasn't unusual for one of them to grab their computer and pull a page up on the internet, ready to prove their point with data. They were always seeking information, always probing, and I was proud.

So, while raising my children was overwhelming, exhausting, and took everything I had at times, they repaid me in joy and satisfaction ten times over. They grew up fast, with two of the three already in college. Zoey is studying broadcasting at the University of Miami and has a keen interest in the law. Zach is attending Rice University in Houston, where he's taking classes in philosophy, chemistry, psychology, and history. He is fluent in French and has plans to someday move to a French-speaking country. My youngest, Zia, is a student at Western Reserve Academy in Hudson, Ohio, where she is exploring her independence as a boarder, playing varsity soccer and running track. While I miss having her at home, I am grateful to still see her weekly and I'm thrilled she's experiencing young adulthood.

When my kids come home on school breaks, they walk straight through the front door of their childhood home in Cleveland to hug our new puppies, Zoso and Zander, the newest additions to the family after the recent passing of our beloved Zilli. Then, with a quick hug for me, they'll run up to their caves to do who knows what. I know that they are happy to be home. Watching the three of them participate in family dinner banter as unique individuals or just seeing them go the extra mile with our dogs, I smile to myself with a sense of pride and satisfaction that I am proud to call myself their mom. A mom who fought through the obstacles of balancing motherhood, work, and love.

Full Circle

While I've enjoyed my stroll through the past, I'm ready for the future with Walker & Dunlop. I firmly believe that selling a controlling interest in Zelman & Associates secured the legacy I toiled to build over decades of hard work, and I know I have found a better ally for this new phase of my journey. I'm excited to dig into the work and explore how our platforms best complement one another to bring a refined service proposition to a wider audience than ever before. I'm itching to get out there and make this partnership as strong as it can be. I've also recently taken positions on several boards and am excited to experience a new part of the business world in that regard. My interest primarily lies in start-ups or companies that are privately held that have plans to eventually become public. Once again, I seem to find myself learning how things work while simultaneously doing them; I wouldn't have it any other way.

I treasure the life I have built for myself, and I am grateful for the security and stability I am able to offer my children. It has been decades since my ferocious work ethic was driven by not only determination, but also by fear. Yet I remember all too well how it felt to be setting out into the world of adulthood entirely on my own. I remember how it is to put in more hours than seems humanly possible, only to feel like you're hardly scraping by. This is part of what drives my compulsion to help people. From the beginning, I've truly felt a need to give every email I've received over the course of my career, even the ones from a stranger or the cousin of a friend whose brother is considering a career in finance, a thoughtful response. But between starting and running my own firm and raising three kids, I never had time to really dedicate myself to paying it forward. In recent years, however, I have been able to ramp up my community involvement in two key ways.

A few years ago, I realized that a huge amount of my passion lies in assisting others to learn about investing in the stock market and creating long-term wealth and security. I have so often come across women and men who are working their asses off to make a living but are afraid to invest their savings because they don't understand the market. I totally get that hesitation, but it kills me to know how much of their stress could be relieved through taking such simple action. At some point, my casual, coffee-table conversations with friends turned into formal financial literacy seminars. They're free and open to anyone who wants to attend. The goal is to demystify the stock market and help people understand that when handled right, it's not gambling at a casino but a way to create long-term wealth. I want to give them the tools and the confidence they need to get started.

My second soft spot is for students. I'll take just about every call from a kid who wants to learn more about finance. Now, I'm not saying I'm a saint. Far from it. I'm not there to be their cheerleader. I recently got on the phone with a college student who was the son of one of my builder contacts. He said, "I'm really interested in real estate and my dad told me you research housing." He wanted to know if I was hiring a summer intern. I asked, "What do you know about my firm?" The answer was absolutely nothing. So, I told him, "For your future knowledge, if you ever get on the phone looking for an internship or a job, do your homework. Know who you're talking to and make sure you're well-versed in whatever that company does." That was it. I cut the call short because if you didn't put the time in beforehand, I'm certainly not going to give you my time. But I can always spare some constructive feedback.

On the other hand, when students reach out to me who have clearly acted to be informed and make the most of my input, I'm happy to help them create a road map of how they should go about pursuing a career in finance. I walk them through the steps they need to take, the books they should read, the podcasts worth listening to, and help them identify areas of weakness they may need to beef up. I don't want to waste either of our time with fluff. I want to get right to the heart of it. I see so many students wandering without direction and I want to help them onto a course that has purpose. Schedule informational interviews early, I tell them. Ask professionals why they do or don't like their jobs. Know about the company you're interviewing with before you walk into that room. Do what you can beforehand to make the most of any opportunity that comes your way. However, even with vocalizing my willingness to mentor young adults interested in finance, very few aspirants reach out with real enthusiasm. There have been notable exceptions with the real standouts being Amanda Young, Elizabeth Sims, and Emily Axner, three young women I have been proud to assist. In fact, Elizabeth is working as a summer intern this summer in NYC for Zelman & Associates, a big step in her career path as a rising sophomore at Notre Dame. Matt Kappler and Kyle Haddon have also greatly impressed me as sales interns reporting to Pete Carroll. The fact that they are from the non-Ivy League schools of Akron and Miami of Ohio shouldn't impact their future trajectory on Wall Street, or wherever they choose to bring their talents and grit.

The core of my passion lies in expanding my teaching and mentorship efforts. I love participating in high school investment clubs and meeting with students on university campuses. I've spoken at women's conferences and at large corporations, sharing what I've learned over my years as a professional woman working in a man's world. There are more financial literacy seminars in the works. Furthermore, I would do anything for young people who are passionately and earnestly pursuing a career in finance because I believe that, if they're humble—willing to be a sponge and ready to learn—they'll make it. When I see that kind of passion, I'm willing to go all out on their behalf. I remember well what it's like to charge into a new field, powered by little more than sheer determination. I am sure these young women and men are tired, and I am ready to extend my hand.

Acknowledgments

Thank you to the following industry executives for all of your support over the years.

Frank Cicero	84 Lumber
Pat Riley	Allen Tate Companies
Ken Balogh	Ashton Woods Homes
Cory Boydston	Ashton Woods Homes
Marvin Shapiro	Avanti Properties Group
Larry Fink	Berkshire Hathaway HomeServices—Fox & Roach
Steve Roney	Berkshire Hathaway HomeServices—Utah Properties
Candance Adams	BHHS—NE NY Properties
Andrew BonSalle	The BonSalle Group
Mark Franceski	Bozzuto Group
Swarup Katuri	Brookfield Real Estate Group
Adrian Foley	Brookfield Residential Properties
Jamers Hecht	Caliber Home Loans
Lee Ann Canaday	Canaday Group
Tony Dwyer	Canaccord Genuity
Ronda Conger	CBH Homes
Don Klein	Chesmar Homes
Dr. Michael Roizen	Cleveland Clinic
Jim Cramer	CNBC "Mad Money"
Toni Haber	Compass
Carol Burns	Compass
Chris Watson	Conestoga Wood Specialities

Dan Schaffer	Cottonwood Residential
David Weekly	David Weekley Homes
Heather Humphrey	David Weekley Homes
Jim Rado	David Weekley Homes
Richard Cisakowski	Distinguished Homes
Patrick Zalupski	Dream Finders Homes
Clark Stewart	Eastwood Homes
Bob Baldocchi	Emser Tile
Mark Casale	Essent US Holdings
Chris Curran	Essent US Holdings
Brian Blaushield	Famous Supply
Bob Hawksley	Fischer Homes
Sandro DiNello	Flagstar Bank
Nick Fink	Fortune Brands Home & Security
Donna Corely	Freddie Mac
Stan Middleton	Freedom Mortgage Corporation
John Winneford	Gehan Homes
Eric Bell	Goldberg Companies
Steve Brooks	Grand Homes
Diane Ramerez	Halstead Properties
Randy Smith	Heritage Carpet & Tile
Nelson Mitchell	History Maker Homes
Bruce Assam	Holiday Builders
Hoby Hanna	Howard Hanna Real Estate Services
Jeff Edwards	Installed Building Products
Mike Miller	Installed Building Products
Jeff Kaminski	KB Home
Jeff Metzger	KB Home
Jim Keene	Keene Building Products
Byron Smith	Keene Building Products
Jeff Brisley	Knauf Insulation
Paul Hylbert	Kodiak Building Partners
Stuart Miller	Lennar
Rick Beckwitt	Lennar
Jon Jaffe	Lennar
Eric Feder	Lennar
Marshall Ames	Lennar
Diane Bessette	Lennar
Allison Bober	Lennar
Sandie Levya	Lennar

Dan Peña	LoanDepot
Jeff Detwiler	Long & Foster
Phil Creek	M/I Homes
Bob Schottenstein	M/I Homes
Mark Spain	Mark Spain Real Estate
Keith Bass	Mattamy Homes
Barry Habib	MBS Highway
Gary Tesch	McGuyer Homebuilders
Frank McKee	McKee Group
Larry Mizel	MDC Holdings
Phillippe Lord	Meritage Homes
Hilla Sferruzza	Meritage Homes
Steve Hilton	Meritage Homes
Jonathan Miller	Miller & Samuel
Doug Smith	Miller and Smith
Steve Richman	Milwaukee Tool
Steve Mungo	Mungo Homes
Vince Napolitano	Napolitano Homes
David Heller	NRP Group
Paul Saville	NVR
Dwight Schar	NVR
Scott Thorson	Oakwood Homes
Brad Hart	OrePac
Tom Duncan	Positec
Dana Hamilton	Pretium Partners
Patti Conley	PrimeLending
Ryan Marshall	PulteGroup
Bob O'Shaughnessy	PulteGroup
Jim Zeumer	PulteGroup
Barbara Alexander	Retired
Ken Jackson	Retired
David Rosenberg	Rosenberg Research
Danielle DiMartino	Quill Intelligence
Rich Maresco	Reico
Barry Ritholtz	Ritholtz Wealth Management
Bob Walters	Rocket Companies
Mark Kroll	Sares Regis Group
Jim Kirkpatrick	Shaw Industries Group
Bert Selva	Shea Homes
John Morikis	Sherwin Williams

Jim Jaye	Sherwin Williams
Dwight Sandlin	Signature Homes
Don Allan	Stanley Black & Decker
Jim Loree	Stanley Black & Decker
Steve Alloy	Stanley Martin
Chris Graham	Starwood Multi-Family
Andrew Miller	Stimson Lumber
Shane Lyle	Strathmore Floors & Cabinets
Sheryl Palmer	Taylor Morrison
Tawn Kelley	Taylor Morrison
Mackenzie Aron	Taylor Morrison
Tom Krobot	TC Krobot
David Drees	The Drees Co
Jill Hertzberg	The Jills
Larry Webb	The New Home Company
Joan Marcus-Colvin	The New Home Company
Leonard Miller	The New Home Company
Melissa Abel	Third Coast Bank
Carolynn Alexander	Third Coast Bank
Doug Yearly	Toll Brothers
Marty Connor	Toll Brothers
Fred Cooper	Toll Brothers
Doug Bauer	TRI Pointe Homes
John Peshkin	Vanguard Land
Rich Rabil	Vanmetre Companies
Joel Shine	Woodside Homes
Brad Berning	Zillow Group

Acknowledgments

*Thank you to the following institutional investors
for all of your support over the years.*

Matt McGee	Adage Capital Management
Tom Cox	Alyeska Investment Group
Matt Simon	Ashler Capital
Jim Rogers	Balyasny Asset Management
Tom Stevens	Balyasny Asset Management
Justin Borst	Balyasny Asset Management
Bob Ax	Balyasny Asset Management
Jeff Runnfeldt	Balyasny Asset Management
Brian Moynihan	Bank of America Merrill Lynch
Michael Ankrom	Bank of America Merrill Lynch
David Kirshenbaum	Baron Capital Management
Jeff Kolitch	Baron Capital Management
Terry Pelzel	Barrow Hanley Mewhinney & Strauss
Eric Gurcharran	Basswood Capital Management
Taylor Banks	Baupost Group
Jack Woodruff	Candlestick Capital
Matt Lentz	Castlehook
Mike Barr	Cross Lake Partners
David Hobbs	D1 Capital Partners
Rob Roell	Diametric
Ricky Sandler	Eminence Capital
Karan Ahooja	Eminence Capital
Seth Shapiro	Empyrean Capital Partners
Chander Willet	FIAM
Holger Boerner	Fidelity Management & Research
Carlos Ribeiro	George Weiss Associates
Adam Hyncik	George Weiss Associates
Ray Azizi	George Weiss Associates
Gary Freeman	Gillson Capital
Sean Butkus	Goldman Sachs—Asset Management
Lee Becker	Goldman Sachs—Multi-Investing Strategy
Katie Corso	Goldman Sachs—Multi-Investing Strategy
Booney Poovan	Holocene Advisors
Bob Bishop	Impala Asset Management
Jason Bernzweig	Impala Asset Management

Mary Dugan	Invesco Management Group
Lisa Sadioglu	JP Morgan Asset Management
Felise Argranoff	JP Morgan Asset Management
Susan Bao	JP Morgan Asset Management
Dave Craver	Lone Pine Capital
Zachary Gleser	Lone Pine Capital
John Koury	Long Pond Capital
Shannon O'Mara	Loomis, Sayles & Company
Morris Mark	Mark Asset Mgmt
Gabe Plotkin	Melvin Capital Management
Emilo Masci	Millennium Management
Bill Miller	Miller Value Partners
Samantha McLemore	Miller Value Partners
Steve Eisman	Neuberger Berman Investment Advisers
James Tyre	Neuberger Berman Investment Advisers
Jason Keller	Oaktree Capital Management
Andrew Immeman	Palestra Capital Management
David Vine	Palestra Capital Management
Rob Pohly	Samlyn Capital
Lew Sanders	Sanders Capital
Monali Jhaveri-Weeks	Sanders Capital
Josh Kirkman	Sculptor Capital Management
Bill Shopoff	Shopoff Realty Investments
Cindy Shopoff	Shopoff Realty Investments
Joe Capone	Soros
Ross Margolies	Stelliam Investment Management
Chris Wilson	Stone Hill
Aaron Cowen	Suvretta Capital Management
Kenny Abrams	Wellington Management
Matt Hand	Wellington Management
Sandhya Douglas	Wellington Management

CPSIA information can be obtained
at www.ICGtesting.com
Printed in the USA
LVHW082009121021
700249LV00014B/390

9 781737 709923